CRIME LAB:
A Guide for Nonscientists

Published by Calico Press, LLC, P. O. Box 6248, Ventura, CA 93006.

Publisher's Cataloging-in-Publication
(Provided by Quality Books, Inc.)

Houde, John
 Crime lab: a guide for nonscientists / John Houde.
 -- 1st ed.
 p. cm.
 Includes index.
 Preassigned LCCN: 98-93035
 ISBN: 0-9658286-2-X

 1. Forensic sciences. 2. Crime laboratories.
 I. Title.

HV8073.H68 1999   363.2'56
                         QBI98-809

CRIME LAB:
A Guide for Nonscientists

John Houde

calico press

For the juror.

Contents

A criminalist at the Scotland Yard crime lab teases out
fibers from the clothes of a hit-and-run victim (ca. 1959).

Foreword

Chance favors the prepared mind.

Louis Pasteur

YOU ARE IN FOR A TREAT as you travel with author and criminalist John Houde through the modern crime laboratory. You'll go behind the scenes as he leads you through the complex yet easy-to-follow steps of a typical crime scene investigation and reconstruction.

This book is dedicated to The Juror. It could also have been dedicated to police officers, attorneys, judges and journalists who will find this book an interesting read. Even criminalists will discover the comprehensive material contained within this book to be a useful tool. Many professional criminalists have focused on their own training to the point of not understanding other areas of the crime lab. The information in this book will be particularly helpful when they have to testify in court, give guided tours through the laboratory or offer career guidance to young, future criminalists. Anything we can do to take the mystery out of our work will go a long way in building credibility with jurors, attorneys and sworn law enforcement personnel.

A few in our profession may take exception to an apparent oversimplification of complex subject matter, but I found the explanations compelling, particularly in light of the introductory quote by Albert Einstein. Turning the reader into a criminalist is not the intent here, but rather to present an interesting book on forensic science without requiring the reader to consult a dictionary and a dozen science books. That's what great story tellers do, and John has accomplished that with this book. Enjoy! And the next time you find yourself watching court trials on television you'll be able to follow the testimony of expert witnesses.

Raymond J. Davis

RAYMOND J. DAVIS is a forensic scientist with over twenty-six years of experience in both private and government crime laboratories. He holds a degree in chemistry from California State University, Sacramento. As the current editorial secretary of the California Association of Criminalists, he oversees the publication of the quarterly journal, the *CACNews*. He also teaches law enforcement personnel in the Administration of Justice program at San Jose State University.

Preface

LAST NIGHT THE NATIONAL TELEVISION NEWS ran a story about a murderer who was convicted because blood found on his shirt matched the blood of his victim. No further explanation was offered. Most everyone is fascinated by the idea of a scientist's ability to match blood, though few understand it. What does it mean to "match blood?" How is it done? Documentaries about detective work and the science of criminal investigation are all the rage these days, but how in-depth can one get in thirty to sixty minutes? One recently aired program glossed over the subject of with a few shots of a large, square piece of film and some dramatic words about how the "killer had been caught by science." How is the DNA test performed? What are its weaknesses? Pose these questions to most any expert in the field and you may wish you had a Ph.D. in the subject when you hear the answers.

The precise language of science is as difficult to master as any foreign language. Though there are many fine individuals who have struggled through years of graduate school to master this language, eventually their ability to communicate without resorting to jargon is lost. They simply can't speak in terms not requiring a translation for the nonscientist.

It is a simple truth too, that the more precise a phrase is, the more awkward it becomes. Try this one: "*In the ontogeny, the phylogeny is recapitulated.*" Now there's a mouthful. In simple terms it means kids tend to look like their parents. Now, it doesn't mean *exactly* that, because the scientific phrase is extremely precise. But we maintain that it isn't necessary to be so precise when explaining a particular procedure or principle to most people. It may even be desirable to be more understandable than precise. If the gentle reader requires more precision, he or she may explore the subject in greater detail, even developing a fluency in the language of science to get the facts first hand. As in any translation some accuracy will be traded for understandability. That's where we come in. We pledge never to use scientific jargon without defining it, and when defining it not to use it in the definition. What's more, we promise to minimize the trade-off between accuracy and ease of understanding.

As criminalists, we are only one part of a larger team of professionals including attorneys, police officers, detectives, medical examiners and others all having important duties. There won't be much discussion about interviewing witnesses or trial strategy in this book; this is the story according to the evidence.

All of the scientific procedures described in this book are real. It may be that no single case would involve all of the topics we must cover so we have taken the liberty of creating a fictional case devised from real situations. We will follow the evidence gathered from the scene as it winds its way through various areas of the crime lab. Come with us now as we go behind the yellow tape.

Solving crimes is far from a solo performance. We are part of a team requiring the cooperation and interaction of dozens of people. I've chosen to use the editorial "we" in order to mask my own deficiencies. If not for the help of detectives, attorneys and fellow criminalists who gave freely of their time and experience this book would not have been possible.

I would like to specifically thank Edwin L. Jones, Jr. for his patient review of the manuscript and for graciously allowing the appropriation of several of his famous cases including the case of the sweet tooth bandit. Loye Barton and Raymond J. Davis deserve a special thanks for their constructive comments and Raymond's delightful foreword. A warm thank you to Frank Cassidy and Vince Vitale for the contributions of case photos, Dom Denio for the FBI's assistance on DRUGFIRE and James Roberts for the bullet examples.

Finally, the only real "we" is the unseen, tireless army of forensic science professionals.

J.N.H.

Introduction

CENTURIES AGO, THE STORY GOES, *in ancient China, a group of men were laboring on a ditch by the side of a road. An argument between two of the men reached its peak when one worker clubbed the other to death with a shovel. The boss, faced with a solidarity of silence after demanding to know who was responsible, resorted to his keen powers of observation. He ordered the men to lay down their shovels in front of them. As time passed, flies were attracted to the traces of blood on one man's shovel, exposing the guilty party.*

What is a criminalist?

Science, as it is applied to the law, has a rich tradition. The Chinese road boss in the story used his "scientific" intuition to find a killer. He may have been our first criminalist.

A criminalist is one who applies science to the law. This professional may be known by the name forensic chemist, forensic scientist or police chemist. The earliest use of the term criminalist dates back to the 1930s where it referred to "one versed in the law," or even a criminal psychiatrist. The term forensic science has evolved into a broad category to include criminalistics, criminology, psychiatry, dentistry, handwriting or fingerprint comparison, toxicology, and practically any specialty which could be used to prove an argument in court. Presently, we use the term criminologist to mean one who studies the social aspects of crime and criminals. The term criminalistics is defined as the examination of physical evidence. Physical evidence differs from testimony or documentary evidence in that it can be observed, collected, studied and interpreted by a scientist using generally accepted scientific procedures. Innovative ways of looking at evidence are not discouraged, just subject to scrutiny by other professionals before a court will allow them to be used in a case.

Criminalistics as it exists today is a young science. Many of the procedures used by crime labs are a direct result of the work of a handful of forward thinking pioneers prominent in the field only fifty to seventy-

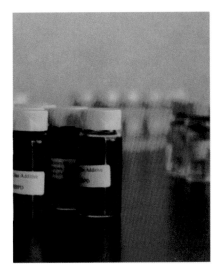

FREEBIES
Samples of automotive gasoline additive await distribution to members of a criminalist's arson study group. Manufacturer's samples are often shared among crime laboratories to keep all criminalists aware of industry changes.

five years ago. One of the early leaders of the profession was a Frenchman named Edmond Locard. Monsieur Locard developed the scientific foundation for what we now call criminalistics, and believed that when a criminal came into contact with another person or place small items such as hairs or fibers would be left by one person and perhaps picked up by the other. His famous "Locard's Exchange Principle" can be paraphrased thus:

> *"When any two objects come into contact there is always a transfer from one object to the other."*

Locard himself probably never put it quite that way, but later authors have condensed his ideas into this principle. It makes sense if you think about it. When you walk out of a room, you've already left behind hairs, breath, body odor, skin cells, clothing fibers—all of which can be termed "trace evidence." That's with just the simple act of walking in and out. In addition to what you left behind, your shoes may have picked up carpet fibers and dust or pet hair may have become stuck to your clothes. Locard went on to suggest that "any behavior with the intensity of criminal activity" is sure to result in a transfer. Finding those particular traces and separating them out from all of the other remnants of everyday living is the real challenge criminalists face today.

Pry open a doorjamb with a screwdriver. If we look closely at the metal and wood that was damaged by the tool, we'll see tiny scratches corresponding to the nicks and wear present on the surface of the screw-

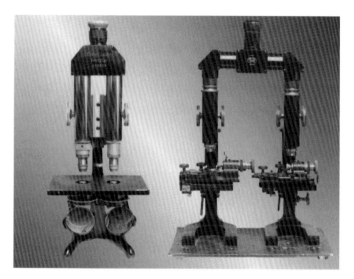

MICROSCOPES USED BY PIONEERS in the field of criminalistics (ca. 1920). On the left is a comparison microscope used by Paul Kirk, probably the first person to use the term criminalist as it is used today. The techniques he originated in the analysis of fibers, hairs and other microscopic evidence form the basis of modern trace evidence examination.

On the right is E. C. Crossman's bullet comparison microscope. Crossman was an associate of Calvin Goddard, the originator of the examination and comparison of firearms evidence. Evidence and test-fired bullets and cartridge cases could be compared simultaneously.

Courtesy Paul M. Dougherty private collection.

driver. Conversely, there may be brass or wood particles gouged from the door and embedded in imperfections on the tip of the tool. In a perfect world, we'd be able to locate and identify each of those traces and prove that this and only this screwdriver made those gouges. In reality, however, an intruder might drop the tool or shove it into his pocket and cause more and different transfers which may obscure the ones we wanted to find. Often enough we'll see scratches on the metal part of the door that correspond to test scratches made by the screwdriver in the laboratory. We don't get that good two-way Locard exchange very often, but sometimes one-way is enough.

Comparing, identifying and characterizing are the heart and soul of criminalistics. We, as criminalists, are constantly comparing "known" objects and substances to "questioned" objects and substances. It could be blood, hair, glass, paint, rubber—anything. A good grasp of manufacturing techniques is an essential background for a criminalist, as well as an insatiable curiosity about the mechanics of the world around us. Evidence arriving at the crime lab is often not in perfect condition. In recognizing the fragments remaining after a bomb explodes, for example, it's helpful if a criminalist has taken apart clocks and radios and timers and knows how they are constructed.

THE FATHER OF CRIMINALISTICS as a modern science, Edmond Locard worked tirelessly in his crime lab in Lyons, France during the early half of the twentieth century. He developed the notion that when any two objects come into contact with each other, traces are exchanged.

For fun, a criminalist might tour a gasoline refinery to see how fuels are prepared, or maybe take a trip through a carpet mill or glass factory. Groups of criminalists will gather regularly to discuss the latest trends in automobile headlight design, because fragments of headlights are often left behind in hit-and-run accidents. Samples of new fuels or plastics or paint chips will be given out like hors d'ouvres at some bizarre party. These samples are jealously guarded and stored at the lab for future reference. All of these things might lead toward the identification of some unknown evidence. Tiny objects recovered at crime scenes need names. Are they relevant or not? If we don't know what they are, how can we answer?

Finally, we want to develop meaningful interpretations from our observations. It won't matter very much if we collect and analyze lots of evidence and then can't conclude anything from it. Professional criminalists don't have a personal stake in winning convictions or acquittals. We only care that our interpretations of the evidence will be correct and lead the judge and jury to make the right decision. After all, that's the real mission of forensic science.

1

Process

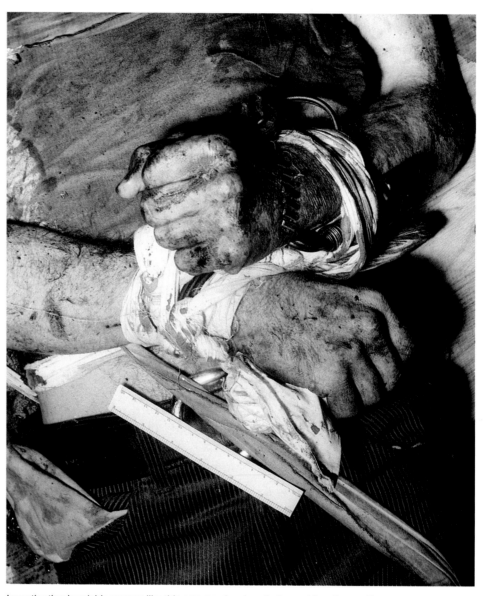

Investigating homicide scenes like this one may involve photographing the position of bloodstains, trace evidence and even the type of knot used to tie a victim.

Let's kill off the main character right now. We'll have to if we're going to have anything to talk about. We'll return to him throughout the course of this book as we learn more and more about how criminalists work. Along the way, we'll show how each specialty area of the lab handles and examines the evidence we recover from this crime scene. Whodunit and why? We'll try to find out by uncovering the truth as revealed to us through the evidence.

THE CRIME

Early on during the investigation of a crime scene, a story about what happened begins to form. It is usually far from accurate, but it does help get us oriented. Victims, suspects and witnesses, not to mention investigators, are all pretty excited during the first few hours after a violent crime has been committed and getting good information can be tough.

Our case involves at least three people: two men and a woman. When the police first arrived they found a man dead on the living room sofa and a woman tied up on the bed in the master bedroom. The woman is conscious and understandably upset. She tells police that some guy she didn't know "crashed through" her bedroom window and grabbed her from behind. He forced her to lie face down on the bed where he tied her hands and feet with some kind of electrical cord. She didn't get a good look at his face and thought he might have been wearing a ski mask. He then sexually assaulted her as she lay there. He sat on the end of the bed and told her that he was going to wait for her boyfriend to get home. About thirty minutes later, her boyfriend arrived and the assailant got up from the bed and went into the living room area, closing the bedroom door. She heard the sounds of a fight followed by the smell of smoke. After waiting for what seemed like an eternity, the fire department arrived followed by police. A neighbor had called for help after he had seen smoke coming from the open front door.

The female victim is transported immediately to the local hospital to be treated for a small cut on her left wrist and to have sexual assault evidence collected.

Who's the boss?

In some jurisdictions criminalists are in charge of the crime scene. Police officers provide security and interview witnesses, but the one responsible for collecting and preserving evidence is the criminalist. In other jurisdictions, the criminalist has become relegated to the role of technician, being given orders to pick up this or that by the officers. The duties vary depending on the relationship between the crime lab and the particular police agency present at the scene.

The suspect has apparently fled after committing rape and murder and trying to set the crime scene on fire. The neighbor, arriving first, was faced with a very important decision. What should he do? He saw smoke but the fire had already gone out, so he could have entered the residence safely. We have seen cases where well-meaning friends have "cleaned up" the scene, disposing of drugs or pornography, for instance, so as not to embarrass or incriminate the victim, especially in the case of a suicide. This can make a simple case a lot more difficult to interpret. Luckily, the neighbor only called the fire department and didn't venture inside. Along with the firefighters came paramedics. They checked for signs of life in the male victim and, finding he had "injuries incompatible with life," they abandoned resuscitation efforts and notified the police and the medical examiner. Generally speaking the body is not to be moved until the medical examiner or his representative arrives.

Gradually, a crowd of officials waiting to enter the house grows to a dozen or so. These include a ranking officer, often a sergeant or lieutenant who serves as coordinator over all of the activities and a couple of patrol officers who first responded to the initial call from the next-door neighbor. These officers protect the scene from curious bystanders, looters or

A FLOORPLAN OF THE SCENE shows where the dead victim was found, on the sofa in the living room. Accurate, scale floorplans are essential for reconstruction of crime scenes and are often drawn by professional draftspersons brought in to help in the investigation.

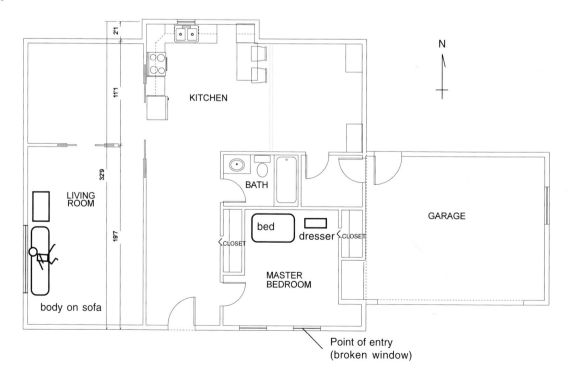

the news media. Later there will be a deputy district attorney or his investigator, but usually these two get involved after an arrest is made. It's helpful when a deputy district attorney comes to the scene since he or she can provide considerable advice about what procedures to follow in searching the scene and interrogating witnesses. Using proper methods in the beginning can save lots of agony later in court. Search and seizure can be complicated by many situations, including a roommate's expectation of privacy or if there was a barricaded suspect still inside the house, or if the recently extinguished fire rekindles. To update crime lab personnel and detectives, the district attorney's office provides training sessions to discuss new laws governing the policy on searching a residence.

Helping us out at the scene is a crime scene technician who will videotape the entire scene during our initial "walk-through." We have been dispatched from the lab several hours after the crime was first reported and we bring a kit full of equipment including precision tweezers, vials of varying sizes, gloves and even a magnifying glass or two. One detective is there, another off looking for witnesses around the area. If our victim had lived long enough to make it to the hospital, an officer would have been sent to talk to the victim's family or even get a dying statement from the victim himself. A medical examiner's investigator will arrive shortly with a plastic body bag and gurney to transport the body to the morgue. As long as we don't alter anything before the medical examiner arrives and since the female victim has graciously consented to her home being searched, we can have a look around and get an overall impression of the place.

Large crime scenes may even have a "scribe" whose sole task is to keep a log of every person who enters or leaves the scene. A public information officer may also be on hand to answer questions from reporters. Burning buildings or hostage situations involve dozens or more people including traffic control, utility workers for water, power and phone, an incident command center staffed with support personnel with cellular telephones and fax machines, and maybe even some Red Cross volunteers to provide food and shelter. It could start to look more like a disaster scene than a crime scene. No doubt every crime scene is a disaster for someone, it's only a question of scope.

Each person present has been trained to do a specific job and as soon as the photos and video are taken, it's time for us to move in and examine the overall scene. We work methodically, proceeding from room to room, saving the area of the body for last. We are always asking ourselves, "What happened here? What was everyday life like here? What does this place look like normally?" We have to sort out life's normal disorganization from the sudden chaos of crime. It's physically tiring and emotionally draining to work a homicide scene. A box of sandwiches brought in by a sympathetic fireman or detective is welcomed.

The master bedroom

When we look in the room where the woman said she was tied up and forced to have sex, we see the sheets and covers have been pushed over to the side of the bed revealing the bare mattress. We collect all of the bedding, carefully folding it and sealing it in a large paper sack. Since the sheets and blankets are already mixed together there's little to be gained by separating them here. Next to the bed is a dresser having a dusty top surface. A clean circular area about six inches across is very obvious. On the floor we see a lamp with a circular base of about the same diameter as the dust-free circle on the dresser. The electrical cord has been pulled out and there are a few wires sticking out.

We "roll" the mattress itself with sticky tape to collect hairs and fibers. We like to go over anything of interest with sticky tape attached to a plastic roller. These tape lifts will collect thousands of tiny particles that will need to be examined later under a microscope.

Looking around the room we notice shards of broken glass from the window. We will take a few to use as comparison samples. On second thought, let's take all of the glass fragments. If we're lucky there might be fingerprints. Also, going through broken glass is risky, people often get small cuts that they don't notice in the heat of battle, leaving blood behind. The frame of the window is aluminum, and has a smooth, dull silver appearance. What catches our eye is a small dent, about a half-inch long on the inside edge. We'll ask to have the frame unscrewed and removed for a closer examination. It may turn out that whatever was used to break the glass also left a telltale mark on the metal.

Checking the map

Since sexual assault is suspected at the scene, we'll make a chemical "map" of the mattress to look for semen. Some crime scene technicians think that simply running an ultraviolet (UV) light over the area will reveal the presence of semen stains. That doesn't always work, but by using a chemical called MUP * we can find semen stains for sure. MUP reacts with the enzymes (biological compounds that help reactions to occur) in semen to form a substance that lights up very brightly under the UV light. If we saw that effect, we'd cut out a section or take the whole thing to the lab to be frozen and preserved. Dried semen is hard to see without chemical help and yet can be powerful evidence. For one thing, it's loaded with DNA. For another, it may be clearly inappropriate to the area it's found, such as in a baby's crib.

Here in the bedroom, nothing is seen on the MUP map of the mattress, perhaps because the assault took place on the sheets or blanket. We'll check those when we can spread them out at the lab.

Incidentally, another body fluid, saliva, has different enzymes which can be mapped as well. When saliva dries it's invisible, but its presence can be important. For example, we worked a case where a police officer was accused of spitting on a suspect. When the suspect's garments were mapped for saliva, it was discovered that he was lying; there was none to be found except the normal spatter everyone has on his or her front garment from talking and eating. When we looked at the officer's shirt, we found a large saliva stain on the back shoulder area. It began to look like the suspect was the one who did the spitting.

In the case of saliva mapping, a UV light isn't used but instead we take advantage of saliva's ability to digest starch. Even though enzymes may dry out, they can become activated again when they are moistened. To map a saliva stain, we first wet down large pieces of absorbent paper, similar to giant paper towels, with water. This paper has been pretreated with starch. When we press the paper down over the area to be mapped, any enzymes present will dissolve into the paper. Iodine is then sprayed on the paper and a blue color develops where it reacts with the starch. If saliva is present the area will remain white, showing a pattern of staining. We never spray developer chemicals directly on the evidence. Even though it would also show the location of the stain, it would alter the evidence forever and might prevent us from performing other testing on the material.

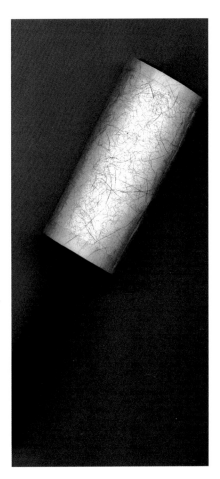

CRIMINALIST'S HELPER
A lint pickup roller with its large area of sticky tape is an effective collector of trace evidence. Only the topmost layer of debris at a crime scene is collected by tape lifts, a vacuum cleaner usually recovers too much.

Clearing up confusion

We want to know a few things right off, such as *how did this person die?* If it was by his own hand, it's the end of the story—at least for the

*methylumbelliferyl phosphate

crime lab. Occasionally we will be asked to verify a theory of suicide by proving a particular gun was used, for example, but basically the case is closed. If death was at the hand of another, we need to find out as much information as possible. Perhaps the evidence will show the killing was clearly justified, such as in self defense. Of course the more murky the details are, the more likely it will be treated as a suspicious death and will need to be thoroughly investigated. Since we are investigating a murder scene, we need to be looking for a weapon. Most of the time it is obvious whether we will be searching for a gun, a knife or a club, but this is not always true. More than one weapon could be involved or none at all. Sometimes a blood trail will lead us to other areas in the house, perhaps to the kitchen where the suspect washed off blood. Maybe old bloodstains are found indicating that this wasn't the first time violence occurred here. The shape and spacing of the drops of blood can indicate how fast a wounded party was moving, so the shape of each drop must be carefully measured and photographed. Tiny blood droplets can give away how many blows a bludgeoning victim sustained or how close the victim was to another object when blood was shed.

The house

We look up, down, all around; nothing is taken for granted. No two scenes are ever exactly the same, but they do share similarities. In this case there is blood all over the place, typical of a violent struggle. There are large drops of blood leading from the body to the kitchen, with a small pool of blood on the floor next to the sink. A bloody towel is in the sink. We see smears of blood on doorjambs, faucet handles, kitchen sink, doorknobs, a telephone and, of course, in a coagulating pool under the body. We see small spatters of blood even on the ceiling above the dead victim. As criminalists, it is our job to decide which samples would yield the most information.

At first we know so little about the incident that we have to rely on instinct and experience. We have to take enough evidence to prove a theory we haven't yet heard to convict a person that hasn't been identified yet, but not much more. There's a physical limit on just how many parts of a house we can fit into the property room back at the crime lab. In one case, detectives had done a beautiful job of photographing a bloodstain pattern on a wall where a victim had been shot. Then they said the heck with

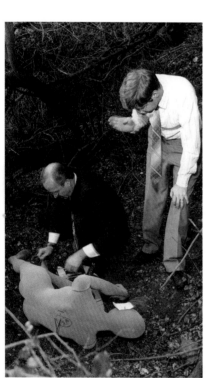

Los Angeles Times photo/Carlos Chavez

CRIME SCENE RECONSTRUCTION
At a remote crime scene, the author (*standing*) and a district attorney's investigator prepare for a jury visit by placing a mannequin in the same position as a murder victim. The defendant stood by in chains while the jurors each filed through the area where the body was discovered.

it, and sawed a huge section of the wall out and brought it to the lab. The property room personnel scrambled to find room to store such a huge exhibit. The trouble was, the mist-like blood spatters typical of gunshot wounds were highly indicative of where the victim's head had been, so we had to haul the wall back to the house to fit it back together and to perform our reconstruction so that the whole scene could be viewed.

Photography is an essential part of any crime scene investigation. It would seem pretty simple to get some film and a camera and go to the scene and take pictures. If we just wanted to record the scene for posterity that would be fine. However, few things get picked over more carefully by lawyers than photographs, and it is crucial to take not only lots of photos, but well lighted, accurate photos depicting the scene exactly as it was found. For instance, every textbook ever written on the subject of crime scene photography shows how to take accurate photos of tire tracks. The camera must be mounted on a tripod and be exactly perpendicular to the track with the lighting from the side. A ruler or scale must be included in the shot so that the photo can later be enlarged 1:1 or actual size. This allows us to compare a suspect's actual tires with the photos of the track. We also might make casts of the track using plaster of Paris.

The man

This crime scene is a nasty one, with a rape in one room, an arson attempt and a dead body in another. The man is lying crumpled on the sofa. The left side of his head is depressed amid a great deal of blood. On the wall and blinds behind him is a horrific blood spatter pattern, looking rather like a sunburst of blood blossoming outward in every direction. A few blood stains appear clear across the room. One detective quickly concludes that the man had been shot in the head. He remarks, "Why I've seen dozens of these shootings, and this is what they look like."

Well, he hadn't seen *this* one, and as the scene is examined further, it becomes apparent that the blood spatter was caused by a bloody object being repeatedly used by an assailant to strike the victim's head. Each time the weapon was raised for another blow, blood was thrown or cast off by centrifugal force, landing on the wall, ceiling and even across the room. It was a vicious bludgeoning—no gun had been fired. Wouldn't the woman have mentioned hearing a shot? What had been a clear case of a gunshot wound to one detective was found to be nothing of the sort.

Truly, no two scenes are ever exactly alike. The wider the variety of experiences a criminalist has had, the more effective he or she will be at determining what happened.

When the medical examiner gives us the go-ahead, we carefully roll wide sticky tape over the dead man's clothes and shoes, saving each section of tape carefully, noting the exact area we touched. When the medical examiner turns the body over we tape the back surfaces. Each square of tape is carefully removed from the roller and flattened out on a clear plastic sheet to be examined later. We can see through the plastic without touching the debris picked up on the tape.

In a dead person, blood settles to the lowest parts of the body. The blood then coagulates and remains in those areas even if the body is later moved. The purplish marks seen in the skin from this settled blood are termed lividity. If a body is moved before the police arrive, the lividity may not agree with the adjusted position of the body. The dead victim has lividity in his lower extremities and feet. When the lividity is compared together with the blood spatter pattern behind him, it doesn't appear that the man had been moved since death occurred. While the deputy medical examiner examines the body, we notice a small wound on the heel of his left hand. We'll tape lift this area too, taking careful note of the condition of bloodstains on his shoes and clothing. When the body's taken to the morgue, it may shift around causing new and unrelated stains to appear. Lastly, we'll place paper sacks over his hands to protect any evidence under his nails from getting lost.

Recording the scene

After the scene has been photographed and videotaped, the locations of individual items of interest are marked by numbers which are printed on four-inch yellow plastic squares. These squares are placed next to objects and are highly visible in photographs. The whole scene is re-photographed with these numbers to clearly identify certain items of evidence before they are collected. A common mistake of rookie photographers is to just focus on items of interest, say, a blood spot on the carpet. An overall shot of the larger area that includes the spot must also be taken. Later, when the photos are examined, after the scene has been cleaned up, it may become important to know where in relation to the victim the blood spot was found. If no overall picture includes that spot, we are lost. We can't take too many photos. Film is cheap, and no one ever regretted taking too many pictures.

We'll also draw a sketch of the scene in addition to photographing it. The sketch represents a particular focus of the scene and is not intended to replace photography. When we sketch, we can make walls disappear or eliminate house plants and other distractions in order to highlight the intended subject. Also, we'll draw a floorplan to indicate exactly where we collected each piece of evidence and show the relationship of the victim to the furniture.

Bag and tag

Most people can recognize blood when they see it. There are a few kinds of food and some cosmetics that could be mistaken for blood, though, so we need to be more confident than the average person. A dark reddish speck seen on the wall could be blood and to test it we touch it with a moistened cotton-tipped swab. Then we touch the swab to a piece of chemically treated paper that quickly turns blue when blood is present. This test is not completely specific for blood, but it quickly rules out most of the common substances normally found in a home.

Now that we've identified areas that look like blood in various locations around the house, we need to collect samples. We don't know whose blood might it might be. The attacker could have cut himself going in through a window, during the struggle or even while leaving in a panic. It looks like the assailant tried to apply a little first aid at the kitchen sink, or maybe he washed off a weapon. If necessary we could even take the sink traps to look for blood in the water that accumulates there. Appropriate blood collection materials are chosen depending upon what testing will be done. Cotton swabs or tiny squares of cloth, called swatches, will be used to soak up samples of blood and sometimes dried blood can be scraped directly into a small envelope or folded paper.

Along with each blood sample or suspected blood sample, we must collect a control sample. This is a swabbing of an area near the bloodstain, but without any blood. We must be convinced that the background material does not interfere with our testing. Ordinarily, things like wood, paper and painted surfaces are not a problem. Occasionally we'll run into something such as leather, food, leaves or soil or some other substance that has particular chemical properties of its own that might cause an interference.

There is a bloody print on the doorjamb of the bedroom that could turn out to be the best evidence in the whole case. Even typing it for DNA would not be as useful as finding out that the print belonged to the suspect. It's one thing to have your fingerprint found at a crime scene, quite another to have your fingerprint in the victim's blood found there. We must decide whether the print is going to be better than the blood alone, since swabbing the blood would destroy the print. We'll photograph it, then, using a saw, cut a section including the print out of the doorjamb and take it back to the lab. There, we'll have a fingerprint specialist examine it and decide if it's clear enough to compare with a suspect's prints on file. We don't generally like to destroy people's property to get evidence, but we have a responsibility to do whatever it takes to collect meaningful evidence.

In addition to collecting body fluids, we'll search through the wastebaskets looking for a store receipt—perhaps someone followed the victim home from the store—or drug paraphernalia. The answering machine will be played back and the last number dialed will be recorded. We have access to our own cellular phones to avoid using the victim's phone for official purposes. Detectives have most of the chores of sorting through personal effects, while the task of recovering body fluid evidence, hairs fibers, glass, bullets, toolmarks, shoe prints and so on is left to the criminalist. It always helps to have as many pairs of eyes as possible looking for anything out of the ordinary.

Even the most thorough job of searching may not turn up many clues. One case we worked that remains unsolved involved a woman found dead on her living room floor. She had been gagged with duct tape. No blood had been shed, no forced entry, no sexual assault, not much of anything out of the ordinary, save her dead body. Several twenty-dollar bills were sticking out of her purse from a recent trip to the bank. While we were working, her answering machine suddenly activated, her recorded voice floated out, "*I can't come to the phone right now....*" Well, at least it didn't say she was tied up at the moment. We searched the house, the garage, the garbage, everything. Years have gone by and we still don't know who killed her.

Getting it all

That pool of blood under the male victim may actually be the best sample we're going to get for some tests, so we'll collect a little of it while we can. As unlikely as it sounds, a dead body might not have enough blood for a good sample by the time an autopsy is performed. Head wounds are notorious in that the heart may continue to pump out blood until there's practically none left in the body. Too often, a few measly drops are sent back from the medical examiner only to be greedily pounced upon by the alcohol, toxicology and blood typing sections of the lab. Each of these three sections of the crime lab want an adequate sample to perform their tests. We'll leave the samples obtained at autopsy for the alcohol section, since being volatile, alcohol wouldn't be appropriately collected from a pool of blood. Toxicology (drug analysis) can often gain useful information from organs and other fluids, so they don't require a sample from the scene. The blood typing section uses blood from the victim to compare to any found on a suspect's clothing or a weapon. With so much blood having been shed in this case, we're hoping the suspect got some on him during a struggle.

The burned areas in the living room are fairly small, only about a foot in diameter. There is a burned area in the carpet and one on the sofa next to the body. It looks like a halfhearted attempt to cover up the crime with fire. Of course, if the woman had been still in the bedroom when the house burned down, we'd have a double homicide on our hands. Samples of the burned material are cut out and sealed in clean metal cans that resemble paint cans. Our cans have never held anything before, so they'll be suitable for collecting evidence that might evaporate. We'll also collect comparison samples from the unburned part of the sofa and carpet. We'll try to find a chemical difference between the comparison samples and the burned evidence because it might mean a flammable liquid was used to start a fire.

Getting it right

As criminalists, we want to find out what actually happened at the crime scene and to be sure that the conclusions we reach are meaningful and correct. If our findings suggest a particular scenario, we want to be confident that the evidence supports it. Usually only one person knows for sure what happened, but he isn't talking. It is gratifying when a defendant confesses as to how he committed a crime. We listen very carefully to what he says because this is when we will see if our scene reconstruction abilities are sharp. We assume what he says is true, but every detail he admits is compared to the evidence. Victims can also be a great help if they survive.

There was a case where a rape occurred in the carpet-lined bed of a pickup truck. We performed our semen mapping procedure, finding numerous semen deposits. Samples of each area were cut from the carpet and examined under a microscope. Cells which are normally found in the lining of the female reproductive tract were observed in only two separate areas of the carpet, each mixed with semen. Without knowing the details of our findings, the suspect admitted that he'd had intercourse with the victim twice. He pointed out two different places on the carpet, roughly corresponding to the areas we sampled. His unknowing confirmation of our findings made our day.

Surrounding the scene

"High profile" crime scenes carry with them additional stresses. There are hours of slack time, waiting for search warrants, waiting for the medical examiner. When the news media arrive they are restless. They want action, movement, something—anything. At one homicide scene the media had been restricted to an area about 150 feet beyond the place where the body of a popular woman had been found. There were dozens of TV crew members, reporters and assistants milling around and setting up cameras. When a criminalist or police officer went to his car for more film, a smoke, a soda or whatever, the TV crews sprang into action leaping up to their cameras, with the reporters assuming their position in front, narrating the scene: *"As you can see behind me . . . ."* They simply couldn't stand the inactivity, so they waited like nervous cats ready to pounce at any movement. A few months later, when the whole jury in the subsequent murder trial was brought out on a bus to view the scene, an enterprising young television reporter surreptitiously placed a wireless microphone in the bushes near where she knew the criminalist would be talking to the prosecutor. Spotting it just in time, the criminalist silently pointed it out to everyone before they could be overheard.

Out of sight, out of mind

After we're done "processing" the scene, as it is called, we step back and think about what we have forgotten. Do we have enough evidence to

Historical Picture Archive/Corbis

CARTOON OFFICIAL
This political cartoon from 1826 depicts the coroner as a bureaucrat who cared little about science. The caption reads, *"Juror: The man's alive Sir, for he has open'd one eye. Coroner: Sir, the doctor declared him dead two hours since and he must remain dead sir. So I shall proceed with the inquest."* Coroners in some jurisdictions are not doctors but elected or appointed officials. In other locales cause of death determinations are performed by doctors trained in pathology, called medical examiners.

compare our findings with a suspect, should one become arrested? Even though the scene will be sealed up for a few days, there's never going to be as good a time as now to collect evidence. Did we check the freezer? The dryer? The backyard? It's quite impossible to search everywhere when you don't know exactly what you're looking for, but we must be reasonable and at the same time thorough. After a while we learn to look in areas typically forgotten by hurried suspects. When guns are used, an attacker will often wear gloves, but did he wear gloves when he handled the cartridges, loading the gun in the relative calm of his hideout? How about when he put batteries in his flashlight? Did he wear gloves when he adjusted the rearview mirror in his stolen car? A favorite place for us to look for blood is on a seat belt which automatically retracts out of the suspect's view when his car is abandoned.

Although criminals try to think of everything when getting rid of incriminating evidence they often forget about their shoes. Perhaps it's because he doesn't think shoes will reveal anything, or maybe it's because they become so comfortable that he hates to give them up. There are countless cases where a suspect is arrested days later in fresh, clean clothes only to still be wearing the shoes he wore during the crime. Tiny blood spatters, glass chips and soil lodge in the many nooks and crannies in the soles and seams of ordinary shoes. In addition to shoes, eyeglasses and watches can also trap minuscule evidence and are also personal items rarely discarded by suspects.

From the bedroom we collect the electrical cords used to bind the woman. One most likely came from the lamp and another looks like an extension cord. If they didn't originate here at the house, the assailant may have brought them with him. It's possible that he has used more of this cord at another crime scene. Perhaps we can match it to a tool used to cut it or maybe other lengths of cord are still in his car. Some people tie distinctive knots that they learned in the military or in some other occupation. At the lab we maintain a collection of books describing all kinds of unusual knots. The ones used here are a couple of common half-hitches, one on top of the other.

We gather together

Now it's time to gather up all of the items we've collected such as the blood samples and tape lifts, bedding and carpet samples, anything we want to package and take to the lab. It's nice to have a crime scene technician to help with this part of the work. Each item is carefully labeled, bagged and tagged. Notes indicate where the item was taken from and which way it was oriented when it was found. This will help when the attorneys come up with theories about what might have happened. Each of their theories will be tested against what we found here today.

Major cases like homicides may involve literally hundreds of pieces of evidence and trouble occurs when more than one agency gets involved. The item number assigned to an item when the photographer places his plastic square near the object is often not the only number that object will get. After the item is collected it may get another number from the lab and still another exhibit number when it's introduced into court. This can cause serious confusion, so it's very important to have detailed cross reference lists so everyone knows which object goes with which number.

Each sample of body fluid that was swabbed, be it blood, saliva or semen, must be thoroughly dried before it is wrapped up. Ordinarily this takes only a few minutes, but during this time the sample must be protected from strong breezes or a careless foot. After it's dry the sample is sealed up in paper and labeled. Large objects may be labeled by writing or scratching directly on the object. Some items simply can't be labeled, such as the actual liquid in a sink trap. The liquid must be repackaged in a jar and labeled and sealed to ensure that the sample that is introduced into court is the actual sample that was collected at the scene.

The grand opening

In some jurisdictions, attendance at an autopsy is usually not mandatory for criminalists. Evidence collected at autopsy will be photographed and documented by detectives, technicians and the medical examiner's personnel. Occasionally we'll go if there's something unusual about the case that requires a criminalist. It may be critical that a piece of evidence be handled by as few people as possible. In some jurisdictions a criminalist is required to be present whenever a homicide victim is autopsied. What we see at the morgue can often help us in our reconstruction of the crime scene.

The victim's whole body will be X-rayed to look for bullets and other metallic objects, then his head, chest and abdomen will be opened up for a more thorough exam. The male victim had a massive wound to the left side of his head. The medical examiner decides that more than one blow was inflicted with a blunt, heavy object and that the scalp and skull show a crushing rather than a cutting type of injury. The number of blows is important to us. It may explain the blood spatters on the blinds near the victim's head. It may also give us even more confidence that a suspect should have gotten some of the victim's blood on him.

When the skull is closely examined, an officer with extremely sharp eyes spots something of interest. Almost invisible flecks of blue are seen on the edges of fractured bone. They are only about a sixteenth of an inch long. They are left undisturbed on a larger chunk of bone and preserved for us to examine later.

The paper sacks covering his hands are removed carefully and his fingernails clipped down to the quick. It makes us wince even though we know he can't feel it. Each of these clippings is saved and will be examined under the microscope. The man's internal organs are examined and found to be normal for an adult male. No other disease processes are noted. An apparent defense wound is present on the heel of his left hand. It makes sense that his arm must have been raised with his hand outstretched, warding off a blow. At least that's how it appears right now. Samples of his urine, blood, liver, gastric contents and vitreous humor (eyeball fluid) are collected in small plastic jars. These will be saved for toxicology testing. More blood is collected directly from his heart and placed in a glass tube for alcohol determination and blood typing. Luckily, we are able to recover enough liquid blood from this body to do all of our testing.

Finally, samples of his head and pubic hair are collected, at least twenty-five from each of several areas of the scalp and pubic regions. We'll need these to determine if any hairs in the bedding were his. After all, it was his house. We want to get some of the hairs around the wound since they may give additional information about the weapon. Hairs can show crushing or cutting that may tell us more about a weapon. If we ever do find the weapon there might be some hairs embedded in it as well.

His clothing, shoes and body samples are sent to the lab. We make sure that his blood-soaked shirt and t-shirt are thoroughly dried before we store them to stop bacterial growth. Bacteria and fungi love to grow on bloody clothing, possibly rendering the stains useless for testing. After all of the objects are dried, they will be stored in a large walk-in freezer to prevent unwanted decay and to retard the growth of mold.

2

Blood Will Tell

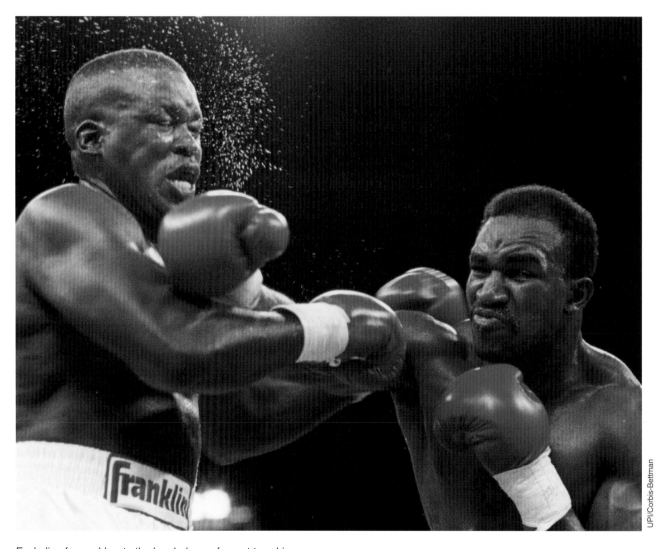

Exploding from a blow to the head, drops of sweat travel in every direction illustrating how blood would fly during a severe beating.

DRIPS AND DROPS

When a force is applied to liquid blood, it produces drops of varying sizes. If a bloody object is struck or swung some of these drops can travel quite a distance. With some simple geometry and an understanding of the nature of blood we can make educated guesses about how the drops were deposited on various objects.

Fresh blood runs freely from open wounds. As a drop falls it forms a little sphere. From high speed photography we know that the teardrop shape so often portrayed by artists simply does not occur. If the drop falls straight down hitting a flat target at ninety degrees, it will make a circular spot. Depending upon the roughness of the surface it strikes, it may burst apart in the familiar star shape with lots of little drops emanating from the center. If the drop hits a slanted target, or if the drop is carried forward in a falling motion, it makes an elongated pattern. The more slanted the target or more forward the speed, the more elongated the pattern. The outline of the elongated drop also tells us in which direction the drop was moving.

Big drops have more mass and can overcome air resistance so they travel farther than little drops. The more force used to create the drops, the smaller they get and the shorter distance they travel. A gunshot, for example, can produce fine, mist-like drops so small and light that they only travel a foot or less. A heavy, blunt weapon can make big drops which could literally fly across a living room.

Absence of evidence

Just as a dry parking space in the rain reveals the fact that a car was recently moved, so does an area clear of blood in the midst of spatter give us information. We can determine that an object was moved after blood was shed by looking for blood that should be present, but isn't. Likewise, if a victim has blood spatter on the soles of his shoes we know he couldn't have been standing on both feet when blood was shed. If we see elongated blood spatter patterns indicating blood moving in a horizontal direction, it's a tough sell for a suspect to claim he was helping a wounded man hold a dressing to his head, and that's how he got blood on the toes of his shoes, for example.

When the medical examiner moved the dead victim's body, there was a macabre silhouette of his head in blood against the white venetian blinds. His head had blocked the blood from staining the area directly behind him. Later, we'll examine the blood drops to see what they tell us.

We had a case where a large, muscular fellow, Larry D., was accused of beating an elderly couple to death. His defense was that he had happened across the old man beating his wife, and in trying to stop the attack, killed the husband. He probably figured we would think he got there too late to help the wife.

In carefully examining his boots the real truth of what had happened became apparent. Hundreds of tiny blood spatters, some less than a millimeter across, speckled his boots from the toes towards the heel. Dozens of them were identified and their direction of travel was marked by a sewing pin with a white plastic head. After a while, a "porcupine" seemed to emerge, a boot with dozens of pins all over the toe, sides and top demonstrating clearly that the direction of the blood was consistent with the wearer having beat a bloody object like a body. The pattern proved that he could not have come upon a bloody fight in progress.

The absence of evidence can make a powerful statement. In the particular case we're studying, the top of the dresser in the bedroom should have been evenly covered with dust, but wasn't. Something circular had to have been moved recently. The clear area is the dust "shadow" cast by the object that had been there.

Once we were working a shooting case where a man, Tony B., had been found dead in a field with gunshot wounds to the right side of his chest. We didn't know where the crime had occurred, but we got a pretty good idea when we examined his car. He owned a compact convertible which was delivered to us at the lab. We rolled a separate piece of tape over each front and back seat and floorboard. When we examined our tape lifts, we saw numerous particles of unburned gunpowder. When a gun is fired, lots of particles shoot out of the muzzle after the bullet. These particles shower down over the area where the gun is pointed. After counting all of these, it was clear that the passenger seat had the most

A PORCUPINE OF PINS was made by placing each pin at the angle indicated by tiny blood drops. This courtroom display was created to show how the wearer of the boot was facing the source of bloodspatter and only about three feet away when blood was shed. Four separate bloodspatter events were identified by examining this evidence.

THE RATIO OF LENGTH TO WIDTH helps determine how a blood drop landed. The longer, narrower stain indicates a shallow angle, while a circular outline indicates a perpendicular impact. The mathematical relationship between the sphere of the blood drop and its projected ellipse makes the technique work.

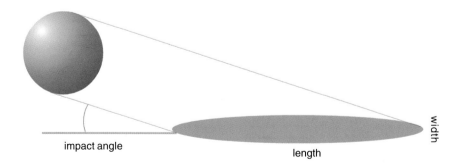

impact angle

length

width

particles. Something or someone had blocked the particles from settling onto the driver's seat. We concluded that the killer had probably stood outside the car and, leaning over the passenger seat, fired into Tony's right side as he sat in the driver's seat.

Could we be wrong? Of course. But instead of a wild guess we have a scenario that is supported by the evidence. We also welcome equally reasonable alternative theories to explain the evidence. Reconstructions can involve something as huge as the crash of a jumbo jet or as tiny as a scrap of cloth. Both require incredible patience and bulldogged determination and can be very rewarding when the pieces finally fit.

Flying blood

We've already described how blood drops leave a distinctive pattern when they strike a target. The shape of the pattern is what we used to determine which way they were going when they came to rest. Picture a water balloon flying horizontally, just above the ground. As it falls, it's also moving left to right. The first part of the balloon to hit is the bottom surface. Because it's flexible and full of liquid, the bottom portion slows down with the friction of the ground while the top continues to travel slightly forward. The last part to stop is the very top. In the case of a blood drop, there's no rubber skin to keep the liquid together, the top part breaks free and pops off a tiny little secondary droplet that travels forward just a little bit more. The whole thing comes to rest as a flat oval shape with a pointed end leading the way. Sometimes there will be a tiny round droplet visible with a thin tail extending back toward the pointed end. We look for these signs to understand which way the drop was moving. The narrow end of the main drop points in the direction of travel.

The shape also tells at what angle the drop hit the target. If the oval shape is long, the angle must have been very shallow. If the stain is perfectly round, then the drop only hit straight at, or near 90 degrees, to the target. We measure the width of the stain and divide it by the length. Then, using a little trigonometry*, we get the angle in degrees at which the drop hit the target. Let's try a few examples from the scene. (All measurements are in millimeters.)

Stain	Width	Length	Ratio	Angle
1 from ceiling over victim	9	9	1.0	90°
2 from wall to victim's left	5	10	0.5	30°
3 from victim's shirt	3	10	0.3	19°

*arcsine (width/length)

Stain 1 was collected from the ceiling directly over the area where we found our dead man's body. It was a round stain, the length and width being equal. The calculations support what we already know, that the drop hit the ceiling exactly perpendicular.

Stain 2 was collected from the wall behind and to the right of his body. This would be a few feet away from the left side of his head. He is facing us, so the directions are reversed for us. The stain was oval and pointed back towards his head. The angle was calculated to be 30 degrees. This is fairly shallow and is a very important number. We can extend a line back from the bloodstain at an angle of 30 degrees to the wall using a piece of string. It crosses directly over the place where the man's wounded head was. This is probably impact spatter created when a weapon strikes an already bloody object. Depending on what other stains there are, we may be able to rule out the weapon as the source of this stain. We'll look at more stains and use strings to see how they lead back to the area over the victim. Stains that radiate outward in all directions probably came from impact, stains that fall in a more or less straight line probably came from cast-off blood. The presence of impact spatter pinpoints the beating in three-dimensional space. It happened right here within the area near the sofa and window blinds.

Stain 3 helps establish the position of the body during the attack. This is clearly impact spatter. It points back toward the head wound at a very shallow angle. Using our string we can extend lines from this stain and many others and see where the strings converge. This is the point of impact or origin for the blood stains. Often there will be more than one

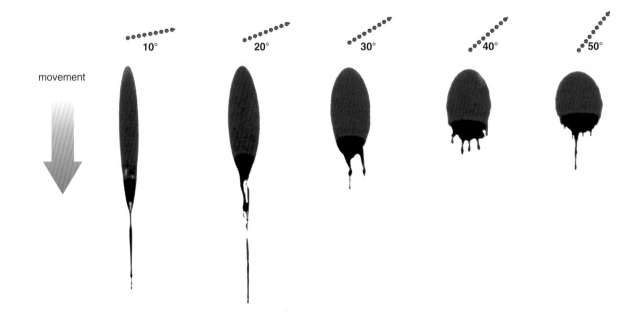

movement

10° 20° 30° 40° 50°

point of origin. It takes experience and a few assumptions to figure out how many times a victim was struck, whether the body moved between blows or perhaps was beaten elsewhere.

We understand the characteristics of flying blood drops from our experiments in the lab. Over the years we have obtained expired pints of blood from a local blood bank and dripped it on paper, hit it with hammers, shot bloody sponges with guns and generally made a gory mess. Then we measured and photographed everything. The data we generated turned out to be priceless in helping us with a crime scene like this one.

Our reconstruction effort leads us to conclude that our dead man was hit over the head at least three times. We base this conclusion on several things. First, we have a rule of thumb, "the first hit is free." What this means is that it takes a first strike to inflict a wound. When skin is broken and blood vessels cut, it takes a second or two for the blood to flow freely. (This is not true for high-energy events like gunshots.) The next strike splashes blood that has accumulated in the wound. The force from the weapon sends it flying off in all directions. As an illustration, we like to describe to juries a picture of a prizefighter being punched in the ear by his opponent. The dramatic way the photo is taken shows the fighter's sweat literally exploding off his hair and face in a spectacular pattern. The same effect occurs when a bloody object is hit.

When we used our strings, we found that they converged on two different points of origin. It was necessary to use a string reconstruction technique on fifteen different drops on the walls and ceiling to arrive at this conclusion. Also, there were two distinct tracks of blood on the ceil-

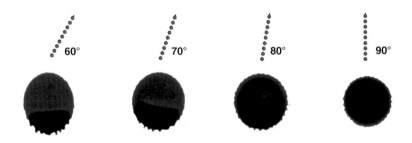

THE SHAPE OF SPATTER
The angle of impact or the forward speed of the blood drop influences its shape. The small red droplets above each spatter in this illustration show the angle of impact needed to produce the spatter pattern below.

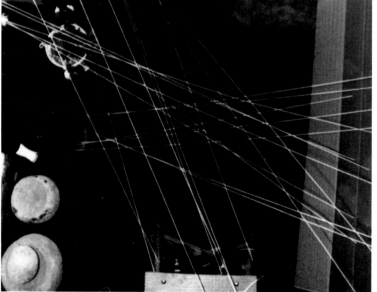

RADIATING OUTWARD and giving directional clues, a large bloodstain pattern *(above)* displays all of the shapes labeled on the preceding pages. Every angle of impact from 90 to 10 degrees is represented. Spatter like this results from a medium amount of energy such as might be caused by a bludgeoning or beating. Close proximity to a gunshot wound produces a finer droplet size than seen here. After the impact angles have been determined, criminalists can stretch strings back to a likely point of origin *(left)*.

ing caused by the bloody weapon being brought back for another strike at least twice. We feel confident that at least three blows were struck, and concede that there could have been more.

We learn early on to expect the unexpected when interpreting blood spatter patterns. Blood in a living person is under pressure and can spurt out from cut arteries making some odd patterns. Sometimes blood will spurt in unison with the beating of the heart and create zigzag patterns across the wall or floor as the victim moves. A punctured lung can cause a bloody cough, expelling blood drops with considerable force, and a simple bloody nose can make a victim sneeze tiny drops which might be mistaken for high energy spatter such as that produced by a gunshot.

An assumption we make when we use our strings is that blood flies in a straight line. This is close enough to reality for short distances, but the farther away a target is, the more the drop falls toward the earth in a curved path. This could make our conclusions about the point of origin too high, so we need to restrict our reconstructions to short distances.

Putting it back together

When people think of a crime scene, they usually picture an entire house or small building marked off with the familiar yellow tape, labeled "CRIME SCENE—DO NOT CROSS." In reality, a crime scene may be as small as the area around a body or a bed or as large as an entire city block. We want to cordon off an area large enough to include anything left behind by the perpetrator. What matters most is preservation. The more untouched a crime scene remains, the more meaningful information it will reveal. What a waste of time it would be for criminalists to examine a scene that has been completely altered by law enforcement personnel and others tramping through.

A case we learned about from a detective in a large city had his people hot on a blood trail. Bloody footprints led away from a dead body, out the front door of a house and down the sidewalk. The blood was beginning to fade as the trail went up some stairs to an apartment. The detectives following the trail were really anxious and nervously knocked on the door, ready for anything. The lady of the house answered the door and wanted to know what they wanted, and why the police kept bothering her; she hadn't seen anything. Two other detectives had already visited her, tracking the blood on their own shoes!

Sometimes the very nature of a crime will cause the scene to be destroyed or changed before we can explore it. In the case we are following, paramedics were called in to attempt to revive the man. They may have moved anything and everything in their way. They cut his shirt and pants to quickly assess his wounds. The medical examiner's deputy dragged her gurney through bloodstains leaving odd-looking wheel tracks in the carpet. These workers are just doing their jobs, but as too often happens, the criminalist is asked to interpret an altered homicide scene.

In another case, a victim was stabbed to death with a small, thin weapon which was never found, a screwdriver perhaps. The investigator thought he'd found the weapon at the scene and excitedly brought it to the lab for us to test for blood. It was a short length of stiff wire about as thick as a coat hanger that had been bent into a handle at one end. We thought it looked a little too perfect, a little too commercially made. As it turned out, this "weapon" was actually the wire guide used to assist the paramedics in inserting an endotracheal tube, to establish an airway. After they were done, the medics had simply discarded it at the scene. We sent the detectives back to keep looking.

Reconstructing a crime scene is hard even if everything is preserved exactly as it was the moment of the crime. Of course, even the perpetrator

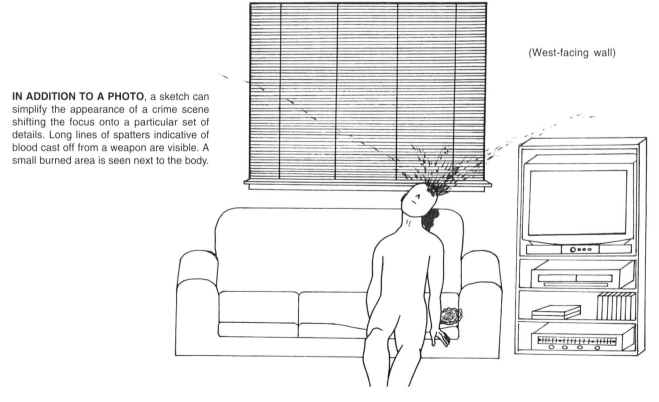

(West-facing wall)

IN ADDITION TO A PHOTO, a sketch can simplify the appearance of a crime scene shifting the focus onto a particular set of details. Long lines of spatters indicative of blood cast off from a weapon are visible. A small burned area is seen next to the body.

of the crime may mess the scene up, either intentionally to throw off the investigation or simply by the act of escaping. Sometimes the evidence itself is unstable and will change over time. We once arrived on the scene of a hot burglary at a golf pro shop, not realizing just how hot until we noticed the impression of a shoe in a vinyl chair seat. The burglar had stepped on the chair to boost himself out the window. As we looked around the scene for other evidence the print just faded away. He must have gone out the window only seconds before we arrived.

Crime scene reconstruction requires that some assumptions be made. We know the laws of physics can't be violated, and blood can't fly through solid objects. We look at the aftermath of an act and think backwards. It's like a puzzle with no answers on the back page but what we see must make sense eventually. It helps to have an inventive, not suspicious, mind.

We are tempted to assume that the simplest explanation for a occurrence is usually the correct one. Remember the lamp with the cord missing? The lamp was probably grabbed off the dresser because it had cord attached to it. The nagging question is always, "But was the lamp really on the dresser?" Well, it probably was, and it could have been. Or, the criminalist's hedge:

"The pattern of dust on the dresser is similar to the lamp base and consistent with the lamp having been there from before the dust was deposited."

That choice of words may sound awkward, but we have to word reports carefully; they carry a lot of weight and could be misunderstood to mean more than we intended. What if we had simply stated that the lamp just came from the dresser. Then, during trial, the defense played a videotape showing a person picking up a cup and saucer from the dresser and then pulling a lamp out of a paper sack and tossing it on the floor. We would be embarrassed by being so positive. Of course the key here is what is reasonable. What reasonably could have happened, not what is every possible scenario. We weren't there, so we didn't actually see what happened. We conclude what probably happened based on what the evidence showed. Sometimes it gets better than that; occasionally, we are able to establish a reconstruction that could have only occurred a certain way. Writing those kind of reports is as fun as it is rare.

3

Scenes of Crime

Example of radial fractures appearing in glass struck by three projectiles. The intersecting cracks can provide useful clues about which shot was fired first.

A homicide was committed by a man who kidnapped Paul B., an eight-year-old boy. The boy had been handcuffed, gagged and sodomized before choking to death on his own vomit. The man then drove Paul's body out to a deserted area, soaked the body with gasoline and set it on fire. Fortunately, a passing motorist saw the fire he started and called the fire department. When investigators arrived, they found a charred little body. Inside the boy's mouth, still unburned, was a makeshift gag, hastily fabricated from a wadded up strip of torn, blue cotton cloth.

In questioning witnesses, the police developed a suspect, one Greg S., a man in his twenties, who had been living with his mother while he worked at Paul's school as a playground attendant. For some time Greg's mother had been suspicious about her son's comings and goings. When police arrived at the house to search for incriminating evidence, she surreptitiously removed some rags from the dryer. For some reason the police never thought to look there. What made her call the crime lab we'll probably never know, but what she turned over to us was a pair of boxer shorts with a large piece missing. All along one edge was a zigzag pattern of damaged cloth. One side of the cloth had been cut, one side torn. By ripping open a seam, the individual threads could be counted, each of their lengths accounted for. The threads formed peaks and valleys which lined up perfectly with the edge of the gag recovered from Paul's mouth. That's powerful stuff, made even more so by the agreement of the total of hundreds of threads. Each and every thread was teased out straight, some long and some short. The two pieces of cloth were smoothed out side by side on a lab examination table. There could be no other reasonable explanation for what we saw. The two objects were once part of the same pair of boxer shorts. A positive link had been made between a gagged, burned body in a field and Greg's laundry.

Now it's one thing to have two objects that sort of fit together and quite another to have two objects that could only have come apart from each other. When two or more objects share similarities that are general in nature, such as color, size, shape, tread pattern and so forth, it is said that they share *class* characteristics. When two or more objects share something more intimate, such as a mutual defect because of wear or damage, perhaps a jagged scratch which runs across each of them, then it is said that they share *individual* characteristics. Most people can understand the significance of finding a pair of shoes in a suspect's closet that are the same brand as those that left a bloody shoe print at a crime scene, for example. But it only means that those shoes or any others like them could have made the print. What spawned shoe print identification as a whole subspecialty of criminalistics was the need to find tiny little imperfections, damage, wear or other characteristics that could eliminate all shoes except those recovered from the suspect as having made the prints.

A piece of furniture may supply the pieces of the puzzle as in the case of a man accused of beating and strangling his wife to death in the front room of their home. During the struggle, more than one glass item had been smashed, including a five-foot glass coffee table. We were asked to reconstruct the table to see if the table had been broken by the victim's head. Investigators supplied us with a box of glass full of broken glass and we went to work. Slowly and carefully, we pieced over fifty-five pieces of razor sharp plate glass back together until the impact point could be seen, a dramatic jigsaw puzzle which took more than a day to solve. Under the microscope, there were no traces of blood, hair or tissue at the point of impact. Later, the detective offered another, more likely, theory that a heavy glass jar full of coins had been thrown through the table during the couple's deadly fight.

Physical match

The whole notion of individualizing objects and their impressions is only about a hundred years old. Recently, the branch of mathematics called "fractals" has been able to offer a scientific explanation as to why things take on individuality as they break and wear down. It has always seemed intuitive that the more details two objects share, the more likely

LETHAL GAG
A portion of the court exhibit used in the case of kidnapping and murder is shown. The gag in the victim's mouth (D) was matched to a cut pair of boxer shorts in the suspect's laundry. (A)

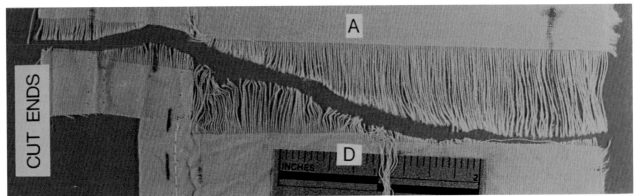

they had a common origin. If it can be demonstrated that the number and type of shared details is overwhelming, then jurors usually find it reasonable to believe that the two objects were once joined together.

Much of the science of criminalistics is based on this idea. Comparisons between tools and the marks left on objects they touch, bullets and the gun barrels they passed through, fingerprints, even DNA are all based on the notion that many objects are similar, but as the number of characteristics held in common increases, the likelihood of a coincidence diminishes. It may be a fragment of headlight from a particular car left at the scene of a hit-and-run. Perhaps it's a chip of paint that fits perfectly back into the jigsaw puzzle of paint chips on the roof of a car. We never know what the "home run ball" might be in terms of evidence recovered from the scene of a crime. It's one of the things that makes crime scene investigation and reconstruction so challenging. A good pair of eyes and an overactive imagination are useful tools to have in our crime scene kit.

Keeping the mind open

Someone once remarked that complex problems have simple solutions, wrong ones. Crime lab shelves sag under the weight of textbooks describing how to interpret crime scenes. One of the most familiar examples is illustrated on the opening page of this chapter. When glass is shattered by a bullet, cracks radiate outward from the bullet hole stopping as soon as they encounter a previously made crack. This can help us decide which bullet hole was there first. This might prove who fired the first shot in a self-defense case, for example.

The photograph at the beginning of this chapter depicts a window pane with three holes. The two small ones on the left were made by firing a BB, the large one under the person's fingers are from a 9mm semiautomatic pistol. What was the order of the shots? It's actually not so easy to tell with this real-life example. The textbooks clearly state that cracks formed by the second shot will be stopped by cracks from the first. What we see in this photograph are some curved, almost perfectly circular cracks from one of the shots interfering with its own straight, or radial, cracks. The upper left shot was actually fired first, the lower left second and the larger hole last. A problem in interpretation is that when glass is not kept perfectly still after it's initially broken, cracks which haven't migrated all the way across the glass may continue to grow in length. Several of the

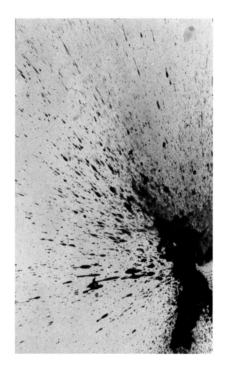

GUNSHOT EXPOSE BLOOD to high energy resulting in thousands of tiny droplets similar to those shown in the pattern above. When sprayed with the chemical luminol, the blood drops emit an eerie glow with an appearance similar to the artistic rendering below.

cracks from the first two BB shots got longer after the shock of the 9mm blast. What is really revealed in the photograph? Not which bullet struck first but which cracks moved across the glass first. Usually that correlates with which bullet struck first, but not necessarily.

Seeing the unseen

Large amounts of spilled blood are easy to see, but finding invisible traces of blood can be as difficult as searching for a hiding suspect. There are no hounds trained for this job, but there is hope. A chemical called luminol (LOO-min-all) was discovered to luminesce (glow in the dark) when sprayed on blood. It is so sensitive it can detect invisible smears on surfaces even after they've been wiped "clean." It must be used in a darkened room, so we often wait until night to use it.

In a rather surprising homicide case a fellow by the name of Greg M. had advertised his Corvette for sale in the local paper. The suspect, one Oscar B., came over for a test drive and tried to relieve Greg of his automobile at gunpoint. Greg took exception to this and after a struggle this customer-turned-robber shot Greg twice in the head with a .22 caliber pistol. Instead of gunfire, the neighbors reported hearing sounds of furniture being moved during the time when the crime was occurring. When we sprayed the room with luminol, the burgundy colored carpet glowed eerily. Up to that point the only blood we had found was on the entry way floor and the walls. To our astonishment, drag marks appeared leading from the living room down the hall. Excited now, we sprayed more luminol. Hunched down in the dark, we stared at the carpet, spraying ahead and practically running to see where these marks would lead before the luminescence faded. First toward a bedroom, then turning around, it became apparent that the killer had dragged Greg's body around the house in a frantic search for a place to hide it. The drag marks finally led to where the body had been discovered earlier that day, stuffed under the bed in the master bedroom.

Luminol also glows when it comes in contact with chemicals known as oxidizers, a common example is household bleach. At the scene of still another shooting, the detectives decided that we should use luminol outside the home where the shooting occurred to see if there were any traces of blood. Windows had been shot out during a gunfight, and we were called in after the area had been swept clear of broken glass. We assembled our equipment and patiently waited for nightfall. As soon as the chemical was sprayed on the cement, we knew we had a problem. The whole area lit up brilliantly. Everything glowed brightly then faded away. Some questions asked of the right people revealed that there had been a small spill of pool chemicals, specifically chlorine bleach in powder form, a few days before. The pool chemicals had been swept up along with the glass, smearing them around the area. The luminol results were reduced to useless entertainment.

Play time

There are infinite variations in the way crime scenes can present themselves. Whole subspecialities have evolved for the interpretation of car fires, for example. There are experts who only look at bombing scenes or blood spatter patterns. After much experience it becomes possible to make educated guesses about why the scene appears the way it does. These guesses could still be wrong, but they should be sound conclusions based upon legitimate observations. A feature of our adversarial justice system is that if one side doesn't agree with an expert's opinion, they may hire their own expert to examine the evidence. It's the jury who must decide whom to believe.

One way to test a theory of what actually happened at a crime scene is to try to duplicate the scene in the laboratory. It can involve things like burning, shooting and generally wreaking havoc. After appropriate safety measures are taken, we are only limited by our imagination. All this and getting paid too! One criminalist used to say, "Sometimes we have to prove that water runs downhill." What he meant was that nothing is taken for granted in court. It is possible that one side may question every little step that was made and demand proof that each step was done correctly. We may be asked to find out whether a car window was rolled up or down when a gun was fired. Attorneys want to know which way would the glass fly? We can go to the junkyard and fire bullets through car windows to prove that glass generally follows the bullet, and that, if the window is rolled down, no glass is broken. Recovering the bullets, we examine them under a microscope for powdered glass embedded in the tip. Can we tell it apart from, say, powdered bone? These trips to the "playground" often yield more information than we first expected. We gather useful data on how far an automatic pistol flings an empty cartridge case, or just how shallow of an angle must a bullet be fired in order to ricochet off, rather than penetrate, a windshield.

See for yourself

It is important for the criminalist to visit the scene whenever possible. This may sound obvious but it is becoming more common for criminalists to work at the lab and let others go to the scene and collect the evidence they think will be important to submit to the lab. It helps immensely in the reconstruction and interpretation of a crime scene to have seen first-hand just where everything really was. It is useful too, for the person who collects the evidence to be the one who processes it at the lab. That way it can be determined how much blood is going to be sufficient for a test, or whether an entire wall should be sawed out to get a bullet.

Scientific evidence is neutral. It shouldn't matter whether a prosecution or defense theory is supported or not, only that the interpretation of the evidence is correct. In a particularly gruesome scene, a fullterm fetus was born into a portable toilet, where it was found dead. On the side of the little building was a spectacular spatter of blood. The case inflamed the passions of the deputy district attorney who viewed the scene. She hypothesized that the mother must have swung the baby in a wide arc, bashing it along the side of the building. After criminalists examined the spatter more closely and expressed doubts, the DA questioned the truck driver of the waste-pumping company, and a slightly less sinister story began to emerge. While trying to pump out the toilet the hose had become plugged, no doubt by the fetus, and the pump-truck driver had back flushed the hose, spraying the outhouse with a disgusting mix of placenta and fecal material. A sad tale to be sure, but not quite as violent as was first imagined.

Clues in the ashes

Arson is a crime in which the crime scene literally self-destructs. Most of the time, due to the expert ability of the fire department, a fire will not be allowed to burn until everything is completely consumed. Occasionally though, there will be nothing left to examine. Several Seattle area fires made the news because of their unusually high temperature. These fires burned so hot that there was virtually no trace of accelerant (something added to make a fire burn more quickly). Through careful investigation, it

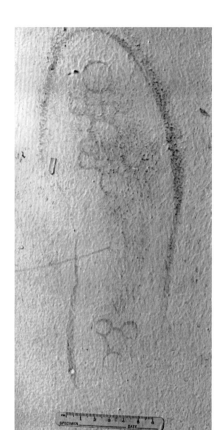

CLASS CHARACTERISTICS
This shoeprint was located on a door kicked open during a burglary. The size and shape of the shoe as well as the overall design of the tread pattern may indicate a particular brand, but class characteristics alone are not sufficient to identify one shoe to the exclusion of all others.

was discovered that a mixture of ignitable metals such as magnesium and aluminum had accelerated the fires. The result was a fire which burned with the ferocity of rocket fuel. After the fires were extinguished, the fuel was completely consumed and there wasn't a trace of how the fires began. Even though no evidence remained, it was precisely that unusual lack of evidence which gave a valuable clue as to the cause of the fires.

Another problem with investigating fires as crime scenes is that the act of putting out the fire is a destructive act. After the fire is out, firefighters have been known to get carried away with "overhauling" the burn. They can do this by pulling out not only a smoldering mattress, but all of the bedroom furniture and heaping it onto the front lawn. One fire crew bulldozed an entire house and then called the arson investigator in to figure out how the fire started, which he refused to do. The fire department doesn't have a monopoly on ruining crime scenes, though. In one notorious case, a homicide victim was discovered in a remote location. Before any tiny bits of trace evidence could be recovered, someone in the local sheriff's department thought it might be a good idea to fly a helicopter over the crime scene—up close. Of course the winds that were generated immediately blew away every piece of evidence that wasn't nailed down, spoiling the crime lab's chances of recovering potentially useful evidence.

Criminalists are known to create their own crime scenes when they can't find one in the wild. Old houses scheduled for demolition are favorite "targets" for us. A single house may serve as a laboratory for observing the effects of numerous different fire "sets." We seek to resolve questions about the quantity of gasoline an arsonist might use, or how much time should elapse before ignition, or how many cigarettes will it take to start a fire in a sofa. What will the evidence look like after it has been burned? Each experiment funds the bank of experience we need to draw on to make sense of a real crime scene.

Crime Lab(rador)

Sometimes a crime scene will be simply overwhelming. It may be the physical size of the area that needs to be searched, the condition of the evidence, the difficulty of access or just the raw destruction. It's times like these that the criminalist needs help. Assistance arrives in different forms, sometimes in special equipment, more personnel, or maybe on four legs. The arson accelerant detection dog can mean the difference between finding and not finding meaningful evidence at the scene of a large fire. These dogs, often Labrador retrievers, have been trained to point out or "hit" on a variety of volatile substances that might be used to speed up (accelerate) a fire. Their noses can detect extremely tiny amounts of fuels and solvents. The dog can't say what the substance is so the crime lab must test and confirm the evidence the dog discovered. In some cases, the dog's nose can actually pick up smaller amounts of substance than the laboratory's equipment. This can lead to a crime lab report of "Nothing Detected" being issued when the dog actually found something. It's not a mistake by either party, just a difference in detection limits. Fortunately, this happens rarely.

In one arson case, a large business burned with a hot, smoky fire. The amount of destruction was huge and spread out over thousands of square feet. Because of the damage, it was not apparent where the fire had started, so gathering samples for analysis became a matter of guesswork. A specially trained dog was brought in, and immediately went to work. Pawing and scratching at certain areas around the burned area, she was able to indicate where samples should be gathered. Subsequent lab analysis proved the dog's worth when traces of ignitable liquids were identified.

Volatile situations

With a few important exceptions, crime scenes aren't usually considered very dangerous. If they occur in an abandoned building with a rotting floor, or out in the middle of freeway traffic, there are precautions which must be taken to ensure the safety of the workers.

"Clandestine laboratories" can be highly dangerous places to work in, however. These are places where amateur chemists try to make illegal drugs by following recipes handed down by other amateur chemists. Their disregard for safety is legendary. The whole scene may even be booby trapped. In one situation we encountered, the final step in "cooking" the drugs involved drying off crystals of methamphetamine (a stimulant drug) saturated with ethyl ether using a hair dryer! This is the same ethyl ether that hospitals abandoned as an anaesthetic a generation ago because of its inherently explosive nature. One jaded detective muttered, "Let's just toss in a road flare and call the fire department."

Only recently has the complete protection and isolation of the crime scene worker been considered. This involves donning the "space suit," a plastic outfit with a self-contained breathing apparatus, and being hosed off with water upon emerging from a very dangerous scene. No one wants to become exposed to chemicals with potentially long-term hazardous effects. It would be one thing if everyone involved, including the suspect, understood what might happen. Then potential by-products could be predicted. But, too often the recipe is improvised if the normal chemicals are difficult to obtain and the results are a complex mishmash of materials yielding completely unpredictable end products, some quite deadly.

Home, sweet lab

Crime labs don't advertise their presence in the community. For good reason they are located in out-of-the-way places far from public view. Buried inside large complexes or tucked away in old buildings on airport property, we try to keep out of view. Security is our main concern. Literally tons of evidence move through the lab and its property room each year. Some evidence items such as cash or jewelry are inherently valuable. Drugs and guns have considerable black market value, although they are more difficult to convert to cash.

We once worked in a lab located miles from the nearest police station. Panic buttons were installed to quickly summon help. As in a bank, pressing the hidden button notifies police without using the telephone. One of the staff criminalists apparently thought help wouldn't arrive quickly enough and kept a loaded 9mm Browning semiautomatic pistol in his desk.

Finally there are bits of glass, bloody clothing, bullets and fingerprint cards which have no inherent value, yet are priceless in terms of the millions of dollars they cost to bring them in. If any of them were to be lost or stolen, the damage to current and future court cases would be immeasurable. For this reason heavy steel doors and video surveillance are used particularly in the property storage area.

In a memorable case of vehicular manslaughter, a suspect's pickup truck was stored in the crime lab garage over the Thanksgiving weekend. We were scheduled to process it after the holiday. As an afterthought, we decided to put laboratory seals on the truck's doors. These are strips of red tape that tear easily, indicating tampering. It wasn't really necessary as the vehicle was enclosed in the crime lab, but we felt a nagging feeling that we ought to take an extra precaution. Sure enough, the following

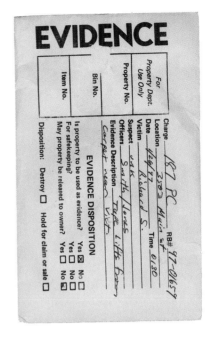

SECURELY SEALED UP
Evidence recovered at crime scenes is kept in envelopes like this one. The back of each envelope *(below)* has a printed chain of custody form where any person opening it must sign and date. Each person signing must be prepared to testify about why they opened the evidence.

Monday we saw that the seals had been broken. An investigation quickly uncovered that during the weekend, a well meaning officer had let in some detectives from another agency at 2 a.m. to look over the car. These fellows apparently didn't notice the seals, breaking them while they did their examination. The now compromised evidence hampered the prosecution of the case. Their activities, while not sinister, certainly reflected questionable judgement to say the least.

Let the circle be unbroken

One of the odd things about working in law enforcement is the concept of chain of custody. Everything we do will be scrutinized carefully by someone else, maybe even years later. It is important to document everything, including who had possession or "custody" of an item of evidence. We must be able to show continuous control over the item from the time it was collected at the scene to the time it is introduced in court. Each person who takes possession of an item must sign and date an accompanying form. It isn't uncommon for a trial to occur ten years after the item was collected. Suspects may flee or fail to show up for their hearings suspending the so-called statute of limitations. When an arrest is finally made, all of the evidence originally collected must be reassembled from freezers and storage lockers. It sure helps if detailed notes were made at the time of collection. If the chain is broken an argument may be made that the evidence was tampered with or altered or even substituted during the period that cannot be accounted for.

Taking stock

The list of all the evidence recovered by everyone at the scene has been prepared by the detectives. Each item has been given a number by the property room starting with the first item received. The numbers are not in the order of collection. This is also the first time we find out the names of the victims.

Turning back to our crime scene from Chapter 1: By talking to witnesses, our detectives have turned up one Ralph P., a man known to our dead victim. Armed with a judge's order, they went to his residence and seized clothing that was similar to a description provided by people who saw the suspect earlier on the day of the murder. Ralph denies any involvement in the crime.

Items submitted to the property room

1. Sexual Assault kit from Lisa W.
2. Richard S., autopsy samples: blood, gastric, vitreous, liver, urine
3. Richard S., autopsy sample: blood for typing
4. Videotape from scene
5. Section of doorjamb with bloody fingerprint
6. Fingerprint tape lifts from various locations
7. Venetian blinds from living room
8. Broken glass from bedroom floor below window
9. Broken glass from outside bedroom window
10. Soil sample from dirt outside bedroom window
11. Blood samples and controls from blinds behind Richard S.
12. Wallet from Richard S.
13. Clothing from Lisa W.: panties, tank-top, bra, bathrobe
14. Clothing from Richard S., pants, shirt, t-shirt, pocket knife, briefs, socks(2)
15. Carpet sample from living room
16. Carpet sample from bedroom
17. Sheets and blankets from bedroom
18. Bathroom rug
19. Bloody towel from kitchen sink
20. Electrical cord from Lisa W. wrist bindings
21. Extension cord from Lisa W. ankles
22. Lamp missing cord from bedroom floor.
23. Shoes from Richard S.
24. Hair samples from Richard S.
25. Rolls of film from crime scene and hospital exam of Lisa W's bruised hands and feet
26. Pillow case from bedroom.
27. Tape lift from Richard S. left hand
28. Tape lift from Richard S. right hand
29. Tape lift from Richard S. chest and body areas
30. Skull fragment with blue substance
31. Rolls of autopsy film
32. Telephone and cord from living room
33. Miscellaneous receipts and papers from waste can in kitchen
34. Bent screen from bedroom window
35. Tape lifts from mattress in bedroom
36. Blood sample and control from kitchen sink
37. Blood sample from pool under body
38. Tape lifts from carpet area around body
39. Sketches of scene floor plan
40. Comparison sample from carpet away from fire
41. Burned carpet sample
42. Suspect sexual assault evidence kit from Ralph P., taken at jail
43. Rolls of photographs of Ralph P. overall body and close ups of hands
44. Running shoes taken from Ralph P.'s closet during search
45. Clothing from Ralph P. taken at jail, shirt, pants, boxer shorts and shoes
46. Can of lighter fluid from under sink in kitchen
47. Burned sofa sample
48. Comparison sample of unburned sofa
49. Plastic bottle of rubbing alcohol from kitchen counter
50. Aluminum window frame from bedroom

4

Perishable Evidence

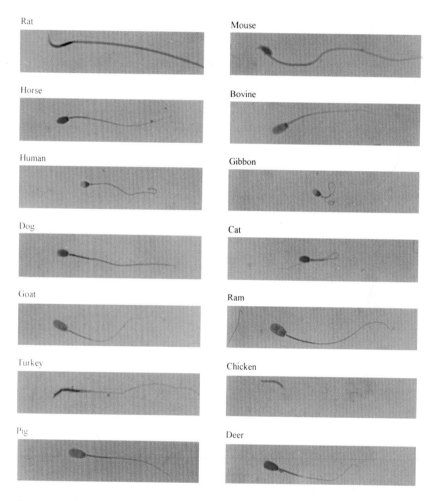

Sperm cells from fourteen different animals reveal the diversity in nature. Each cell is magnified 900 times actual size. These are photographs of specimens prepared by Rodney J. Blach.

It's elementary

Sir Arthur Conan Doyle's mythical detective, Sherlock Holmes, was able to assist investigators by looking at an item of evidence and rendering detailed observations about the suspect:

> *"If you can say definitely, for example, that some murder had been done by a man who was smoking an Indian lunkah, it obviously narrows your field of search."*
>
> (Sherlock Holmes, The Sign of Four)

In the real world we are more often forced to work reactively, trying to associate or eliminate a suspect who's already under suspicion. That's just a fact of life for labs having more cases than caseworkers. We tell detectives that when they find a suspect, we'll be able to prove whether it's the right guy. Fingerprints, semen or blood left behind or taken away from a crime scene may provide a direct link between suspect and crime scene. Associative evidence such as hairs or fibers may tend to suggest that there was some contact between the suspect and the crime or vice versa. Defendants are not required to explain how these things got there, but they often try to. As criminalists we are frequently asked to corroborate or refute a defendant's story.

With their huge fingerprint database, the FBI as well as some state governments have been compiling DNA (genetic information found in the cells of the body) data on arrested persons with the idea of making "cold hits" more common. A cold hit is when a fingerprint or DNA found at the scene is compared against a large database without prior knowledge of to whom the sample belongs. The computer prints out a list of likely suspects and each is manually checked against the sample from the crime scene. The success of the operation depends entirely on the size of the database. It will take years for states and countries to compile DNA databases containing enough information to make this technique more than occasionally fruitful. Firearm information is also being stored in the computer so that soon, laboratories around the globe can share information about guns and even bullet images.

Blind alley

We sent the section of doorjamb with the bloody print to the fingerprint examiners who work next door to the lab. These are the specialists in examining latent (undeveloped) prints lifted from objects at crime scenes and comparing them to inked prints taken when a person is arrested or applies for a sensitive job. Their latest marvel is a computerized imaging system which scans a fingerprint and identifies various points of comparison. A "point" being a feature of the ridge detail on the fingerprint that can be used for identification, perhaps a place where two tiny ridges meet or separate. The group of points is searched against huge databases of fingerprints. The results of the search are always reviewed by the fingerprint examiner before a match is proclaimed, the computer only suggests likely candidates.

Our fingerprint expert gives us a disappointing report. The fingerprint on doorjamb turns to be a partial palm print. The national and state databases don't have information on palm prints so no match was found. The detectives will get a set of full palm prints from each of the three players and request that comparisons be made to this print.

The list grows

The detectives are relentless in their search for a weapon. They have brought in several tools from the homes of Richard (the victim) and Ralph (the suspect). On a hunch that the blue stuff on Richard's skull is paint from the weapon, they've focused on blue-painted, heavy, blunt items made of wood or metal. The items are added to our evidence list and requests for analysis have been sent to us.

> 51. Hammer from kitchen drawer of Richard's house
> 52. Blue wrecking bar from Ralph's garage
> 53. Blue baseball bat from Ralph's closet
> 54. Blue crowbar from Richard's garage

We are eager to start opening packages, but before we start examining evidence, let's brush-up a little in the area of basic biology.

Biology 101

Our bodies are made of cells. A cell is defined as a small unit of life. A single cell could be big—an ostrich egg, for example, is a single cell. By contrast, numerous human skin cells could easily fit inside an area smaller than the period at the end of this sentence. Cells in animals and plants specialize according to their duties. Flat cells which are well suited to covering large areas form skin; cells that contract make heart and muscle. Each cell has a rounded mass in the center called the nucleus where the DNA is housed. The "soup" surrounding the nucleus is filled with nutrients and structures that the cell uses to carry out its various functions, such as making protein or contracting or secreting digestive enzymes.

Billions of cells performing similar functions are organized into tissues which may be further grouped into organs such as a heart or liver. The skin is considered our largest organ. Parts of our bodies which would otherwise be exposed to the harsh elements of the world are protected by skin cells. As skin cells age they migrate to the surface, forming a tough outer layer which gives us even more protection. The cells lining the mucous membranes of our nose, mouth and reproductive tracts are constantly being sloughed off. Day after day, throughout our entire lives, we lose them by the millions, replacing them with new ones. This is good news for criminalists who like it when people leave things that can identify suspects and victims at crime scenes. These cells are too small to be seen with the naked eye and are called epithelial (ehppee-THEE-lee-al) cells.

Jail cells

If it weren't for epithelial cells, we'd practically be out of a job. These little fellows are found in saliva, vaginal fluids, fecal matter and everything that contacts the moist cavities of the body. These are the nose, mouth and all the places it's illegal to touch if the owner says "don't." We worked a case where a man by the name of Gary T. was accused of placing his finger in a woman's vagina against her will. He was sitting calmly in the interview room of the police station when we arrived at the detective's request. The suspect was quite cooperative while we carefully swabbed each finger individually. After a microscopic examination of the swabs, we informed the detective that, assuming he did it, we could even tell which finger he used. We'll reveal how in a moment.

When foreign objects are used to penetrate a victim's body cavities, we can tell how far they were inserted by looking for epithelial cells. We even have special staining techniques that can distinguish between epithelial cells from the mouth and cells from other places.

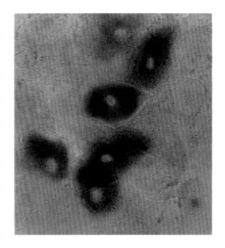

BY THEIR CHOCOLATE-BROWN color, these Lugol positive cells announce their presence. Glycogen, stained with iodine, is responsible for the appearance of these cells not normally found in the mouth in any appreciable numbers. In the background are seen numerous other glycogen deficient epithelial cells which didn't take the stain.

Iodine revisited

In the first chapter we discussed the saliva mapping technique. Iodine was used to indicate starch that hadn't been digested by salivary enzymes, leaving a blank spot where saliva was present. Starch is a way for plants to store lots of sugar. Animals have a similar substance called glycogen (GLY-coh-jen). Iodine combines with glycogen in a similar way, something we take advantage of in the lab. Epithelial cells from the mouth stain differently with iodine than epithelial cells from other areas of the body. We think it may be due to the glycogen being digested by enzymes in the mouth. It's not an all or nothing thing, however, and many cells must be looked at under the microscope. Decades ago this procedure, called Lugol's test, was abandoned by some crime labs because it seemed that there were too many exceptions for it to be reliable. We think those labs made the mistake of thinking the test was absolute. We discovered that by comparing the ratio of glycogen-containing cells to the total number of cells with nuclei, we could tell with reasonable certainty if the evidence had been in contact with the mouth or another body cavity.

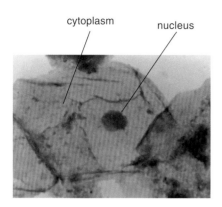

cytoplasm   nucleus

AN EPITHELIAL CELL *(above)* recovered from a vaginal swab and stained to make the internal structures more clearly visible. *Below:* Sometimes unusual objects are seen under the microscope such as this two-tailed sperm cell.

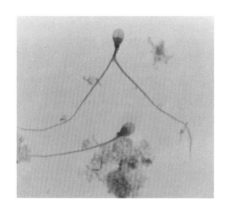

Going back to the finger swabbings from Gary T., we cut a tiny bit off of each cotton swab and placed it into a tube with a drop of water. After swishing it around, we drew out the water with an eyedropper and placed it on a microscope slide to dry. Next we added a drop of Lugol's iodine, a solution of iodine, potassium iodide and water. Under the microscope we saw a field of epithelial cells. For his index finger, we saw about a hundred cells, none of which had a nucleus. These were all dead skin cells, normally found on everyone's body surface. The swab taken from his right thumb showed lots of cells with nuclei. These were living cells from a mucous membrane. None of the cells had much color, though, and probably came from someone's mouth. Maybe Gary sucks his thumb? We continued the process for the other eight fingers.

When we came to the middle finger of his right hand, we counted exactly one hundred cells with nuclei. Of these hundred, we saw sixty-five had a rich, chocolate brown color, indicative of glycogen stained with iodine. This is not normal for the mouth, but is normal for a vagina. The percent can fluctuate from day to day throughout the menstrual cycle and from woman to woman, but in this case such a high percentage could only mean contact with a mucous membrane other than the mouth.

Rape kit

The very first item of evidence we open up is the "rape kit" from Lisa W., the female victim from Chapter 1, after she went to the hospital. The kit is a large envelope containing a variety of items routinely taken from everyone, male or female, when they are examined at the hospital following a sexual assault. The evidence in the kit is perishable and must be examined as soon as it comes into the lab. Some big crime labs get so many of these in a day that they just remove the liquid blood vials (to prevent bursting) and store the unexamined kits in a freezer until a suspect is arrested.

Nurses and doctors who have received special training to examine victims of sexual assault collect this evidence. The examination is a traumatic experience for Lisa, but if there is any chance of linking Ralph to her, this is it. It's essential that a victim report the crime within a few hours of its occurrence, as his or her body will naturally rid itself of anything foreign through the normal flushing of natural secretions. If she waited too long, Lisa's reproductive tract would have eliminated the biological evidence an assailant left behind.

One of the important substances we use to detect semen is an enzyme. After only a few hours it is difficult to detect this enzyme. Enzymes are hardy little chemicals produced by the body that cause chemical reactions to take place. We take advantage of their special powers or "activity," as we call it in the lab, by making them cause color changes to occur. The more enzyme present, the deeper and faster the color change. One of the enzymes found in semen, called AP or acid phosphatase, is practically gone within twelve to twenty-four hours after intercourse. By the end of a that time the levels of this enzyme will be too low to detect. Sperm may last a little longer, but after about three days they're gone too. Note that "semen" refers to the entire fluid ejaculated, not just the sperm cells.

These intervals depend upon several assumptions: First, we assume that Ralph ejaculated a normal amount (around half a teaspoonful) of semen into the victim and no condom was used. The less ejaculate, the less time remaining before we can't find anything to analyze. Second, we assume Lisa is alive and moving about. A dead or immobile victim can hold the semen for weeks and longer. If the suspect has had a vasectomy or some abnormality in his reproductive organs we might also have trouble finding sperm cells.

Tubes and swabs

In the kit we find a glass test-tube of blood. A few drops are removed and spread onto clean cotton cloth to be dried, frozen and stored. We can use this sample for DNA and ABO (blood group) typing, as well as for other tests. When stored this way we can fit thousands of squares of blood samples from many year's worth of cases into our freezer. Later, we may need to send one of these across the country for special testing, and it's convenient not to have to deal with liquid blood.

Next we find a tube of clear liquid, labeled, "*Vaginal Wash—Lisa W.*" The liquid contains a few drops of saline solution used by hospital personnel to rinse Lisa's vagina. There are also several tubes containing cotton-tipped swabs. They are used to swab the vagina as well as the cervix. These swabs usually have the best samples of semen if there is any. They are applied dry or slightly moist, so they aren't diluted like the vaginal wash. Another swab is labeled *"Rectal"* and is a sample of the contents of her rectum.

Timing

One of the important uses for these swabs is to get an approximate time between intercourse and when the sample was collected. As soon as semen is deposited, it mixes with other fluids and its enzyme activity declines. Collecting the rape kit sample effectively stops this decline and allows us to preserve samples by drying and freezing them. Our method of determining the time interval is only approximate, but if a victim claims to have had sex recently, and shows a low seminal enzyme activity, there could be lots of reasons, one of which is that he or she is mistaken about when the assault occurred. Alternatively, if the victim claims the sex happened days ago but the seminal enzyme activity is high, we suggest that he or she is *very much* mistaken about the time of the last intercourse.

More collecting

Also included in the rape kit are fingernail scrapings and pubic hair combings, all collected with the hope of finding some remnant of the assailant. Anything on which the suspect could have deposited body fluids is also swabbed. If the victim had claimed he licked her arm, the rape kit would have included arm swabs, one from each arm. We want one from the area of contact and one from the other arm for comparison.

A somewhat controversial item included in a rape kit is the toxicology blood sample. This sample is collected for the express purpose of determining Lisa's alcohol and drug levels. Since the crime of rape often involves consent, the victim's capacity to form consent is important. Some people feel that it should not matter what the victim's state of drug or alcohol influence was at the time. Defense attorneys could use the test results against the victim, in effect putting the victim on trial. We take the position that if the medical personnel include the toxicology sample in the kit, we'll test it. If we don't find a toxicology blood sample in the kit, we won't ask why.

History, herstory

The rape kit includes a detailed patient history and examination form completed by the attending nurse or doctor at the hospital. We see that Lisa stated that the assault happened about 6 p.m. Samples were collected at 8:30 p.m. That's good, less than three hours. The sooner we can recover this fleeting evidence the better to get meaningful results. The hospital form reports that she did not douche, shower or bathe after the event. In fact she was released from her bonds and taken to the hospital immediately, heads-up thinking on the part of the detectives. Lisa claimed the last time she had consensual sex was a "couple of days ago." This is a very important detail. If the assailant's sperm is not the only sperm present, we may have a more difficult time separating out the suspect from among others.

The examination of her genitalia is negative for trauma according to the medical comments on the form. They use the phrase, "Exam consistent with history." In the case of minors, the finding of semen anywhere is suspicious, the younger the victim, the more so. In the course of our duties we examine crib bedding, disposable diapers, tiny pairs of pajamas. All of the members of the medical and law enforcement team are professionals, but not made of stone, so our hearts go out to these most innocent of victims. At the same time we are glad when an accusation of molestation is unfounded. More than once we've heard of a parent misreading the hospital form and flying into a rage. We'll try to defuse awkward situations by helping nonmedical persons understand that the phrase, "Exam consistent with history" simply means nothing contrary was found, not that there was medical proof of rape.

The routine

When examining evidence we always wear gloves for two important reasons. First, we know that diseases can be contracted from biological evidence and second, since the presence of even one sperm cell could be significant, we wouldn't want to contaminate the evidence with unrelated material. Contamination is a two-way street.

Lining up each of the items removed from the kit, we begin our routine. A tiny slice of each cotton swab is clipped off and dropped in a small glass test-tube. Next, a single drop of water is added to wet the cutting. This is called "extracting" the swab. A portion of that water drop is removed and placed on a microscope slide and left to dry. A fraction of the remaining liquid in the tube is tested for the presence of blood using a method similar to the one we used at the crime scene. A strongly positive result could be due to menstrual bleeding or from recent trauma. To the last bit of liquid we apply a special chemical which turns blue in the presence of the seminal enzyme, AP. As soon as this chemical is applied, we start a stopwatch. A previously run control sample of known semen took only six seconds to turn blue. The evidence sample from Lisa takes fifty-five seconds. We know that a lot depends upon how much material the medical personnel were able to get onto the swab. That's a big question mark, so our estimates are just that—estimates. Nevertheless, fifty-five seconds indicates a pretty weak reaction.

Lisa's pubic combing and fingernail scrapings have no evidence on them. This isn't unusual, but these samples have to be taken just in case. Many of the questions thrown at us by defense attorneys focus on what we failed to do, and what we might have found if we had done it. We have to be diligent in looking at everything.

After a few minutes the drop on the microscope slide is dry and ready to be stained. Cells from plants and animals are clear and mostly colorless, and they need some help if we want to see inside them. When chemical dyes, called stains, are added right onto the spot where the swab extract was placed, different parts of a cell take on the dyes, coloring them and making them easier to see under the microscope. In this instance the nucleus stains red and the cytoplasm (fluid surrounding the nucleus) green. This combination of colors gives the stain the nickname "Christmas Tree stain."

Today we're going to examine the swabs from the victim and look for cells. Everyone knows what a tadpole-shaped sperm cell looks like. The epithelial cells look like tiny fried eggs and are a little larger than sperm cells.

The stains from the vaginal swab make a colorful image. Looking through the eyepiece of the microscope, we see hundreds of cells, each a light green with a reddish nucleus. Occasionally we see a small, oval object half red and half clear. These are sperm cells which have lost their tails. We don't try to identify a tail by itself, but the shape and color of the head is quite distinctive. After this examination, a Lugol's iodine stain is performed. We aren't looking for anything in particular, just establishing whether Lisa sheds epithelial cells containing glycogen and, if so, in what proportion. We count seventy-three positive, chocolate-brown cells, for every hundred cells having a nucleus.

What else could it be?

A complete sperm cell, head and tail, is unique in shape. No other cell in the body looks quite the same, thus its identification is easy. The head and tail can become separated, and there are bacterial and other enzymes which can make this happen quickly, but even some old stains still have sperm with tails attached. When the heads are seen alone we have to be very careful before pronouncing it a sperm. Usually we'll call another criminalist over to the microscope to have a look and render a second opinion. Some yeasts can mimic a sperm head during certain periods in their growth cycle, but our training includes being able to tell them from real sperm.

Sperm cells are tiny but they are manufactured in males by the millions. Their concentration is so high that they make the best marker of sexual activity of all. No other body fluid has a substance even close to sperm's uniqueness and proliferation. A single drop of semen can contain 5,000,000 sperm cells, and an average ejaculation can be equal to 50 of those drops. All we need to perform a DNA test are a hundred or so sperm.

Contamination becomes an important issue when dealing with such a high concentration. For that reason we don't agree with lab procedures which call for dried semen stains to be scraped off of garments and bedding. We prefer a slower, calmer removal with a moist swab or cutting the fabric out in a tiny square. This way, we avoid launching dust potentially containing thousands of sperm cells around the lab and other evidence.

We can and do identify a single sperm head without a tail. In some labs, this practice is not allowed. We even know of one lab that refuses to report the presence of sperm unless they find five sperm heads. Five? Why an object becomes a sperm after the fifth one is a mystery to us. We admit that if a single sperm head is partially obscured by cellular debris or fails to take the stain well, we'll hedge in our conclusion. But if the single cell is clearly visible, unobstructed, the correct colors, size and shape, then we say it's a sperm. We are always open to suggestions from other scientists about what else it could be.

In one case of suspected sodomy, we found what appeared to be several sperm cells without tails. Expecting a stiff challenge by the defense attorney, we searched all available literature for other possibilities. If only it had a tail. We compared it against yeasts, spores, bacteria, pollens, and anything else of similar size and shape. We photographed it using sophisticated techniques and even enhanced the image with computers. Nothing quite fit except a sperm head. Later the suspect admitted to his jail cellmate that he had, in fact, committed the crime.

Tough calls

A serious problem can occur when a medical doctor at the local hospital tries to play criminalist. The doctor's opinion carries considerable weight and is sometimes incautiously expressed. Now and then a doctor will save a little of the vaginal wash fluid and look at it under his or her own microscope. Seeing an object that looks like a sperm cell, he or she may report a finding of semen on the rape kit form.

In one such case, an ambulance transported an eleven year-old girl to the hospital for a minor injury. When she was examined, doctors became suspicious about a vaginal discharge she was suffering from and a swab of the material was collected. When the hospital pathologist examined a microscope slide of the swab, he identified "one intact sperm cell and numerous tails." When the father heard the news he became enraged, convinced that only the paramedics who drove the girl to the hospital could have assaulted her. The father knew he himself didn't do it. If the doctor said he found semen, it must have been the ambulance drivers!

When the crime lab heard the pathologist had identified "tails" we became enraged too; we don't think tails alone can be identified by these methods. After several criminalists examined the slide carefully it was pronounced "clean." There was a suspicious smear on the slide which looked like a sperm cell but was about five or ten times too big. Squashed epithelial cells and smears of mucus can look a lot like sperm, but without the characteristic tail, a sperm cell needs to be specially stained and examined very carefully before it is called a sperm head.

The finding of semen on bedding or clothing is not necessarily evidence that a crime occurred. The very mention of such a finding in court can inflame the jury. We feel an obligation to point out to prosecutors that men frequently have sperm on their underwear, for example. It's even normal to have a few in a man's urine sample. Everything depends upon context though, and the finding of sperm in the urine sample of a female child clearly indicates unlawful activity.

Husbands, wives and lovers

Except in the case of minors or violent trauma, sexual assault is primarily a consent issue, something which is difficult to prove scientifically. We call it, "He said, she said." The lab stands on the sidelines ready to prove who did the act, but if the two parties only disagree on whether it was invited, there is little for the lab to do. There's often a ton of evidence to examine with no hope of resolving the key disagreement. A typical example would be where a man was charged with spousal rape. He lives at the house, so his hair and clothing are all over the place. His semen stains may be legitimately present on bedding. It's an awkward situation for the crime lab.

The flip side of that is the stranger rape. Richard and Lisa were living at the house together, so we'd expect their hair to be all around. We need comparison samples from both of them to be able to spot foreign hairs. Here's where the crime lab really shines. Ralph is denying any contact whatsoever with either victim, so if we can establish a link, he'll be trapped by his own words.

We don't do windows

The crime lab is not a health department lab, so we do not check for pregnancy, AIDS or any sexually transmitted diseases. We can and do refer inquiries for these services to the local health department. We are mindful of the risks to us as handlers of blood and body fluids. Each criminalist has personally received hepatitis (liver infection) vaccine, but

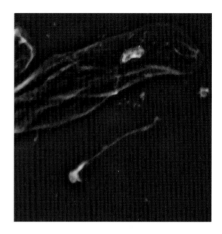

A TRAP FOR THE UNWARY
This smear *(above)* resembles a human sperm cell. The crime lab uses special stains which can easily distinguish this pretender from the real thing *(below)*.

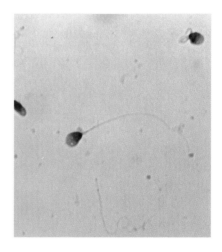

knows that the only real protection comes from using protective gear such as gloves and by frequent hand washing.

Sometimes we get unusual items in the rape kits. Blurry Polaroids of bruised victims, rolls of undeveloped film, urine samples, even audio cassette tapes of interviews are sometimes submitted by the hospital. We just send these off to the detectives and make a mental note to bring it up at the next hospital crew training session. If the victim was wearing a tampon at the time of the assault this too may be sent inside the rape kit. We'll freeze it for future use since it's absorbent quality might have trapped semen from the assailant.

Suspect kit

Soon after Ralph was arrested, we received a kit of his samples collected by a male nurse or technician at the jail. It's an abbreviated version of Lisa's kit. All it has in it are blood samples for typing and testing for alcohol and drugs, standard hair samples from his head, body and pubic region, a pubic combing, fingernail scrapings and a penis swab.

Ralph was arrested the morning following the crime. This could be good if he didn't bathe or shower in the meantime. Microscopic evidence might have been transferred between the victim and Ralph without his realizing it. We find two hairs in the pubic combing which we'll save and compare to his hair standards later. People shed their own hairs, so we won't jump to any conclusions.

The penis swab is sampled and extracted just like the vaginal swabs. A microscope slide is prepared the same way, too. When we examine the stained slide under the microscope, we see numerous dead epithelial cells, none of which have a nucleus. There's no need to try the Lugol's test on this swab, since it is only valid for nucleated cells. Essentially the test is negative for the presence of vaginal epithelial cells.

We are subdividing the items of evidence as we open each package. We number things with letters like 1(a), which would be the blood sample out of Lisa's rape kit or 1(b) which would be the toxicology/alcohol blood sample also out of item 1. The total number of items in the case will probably double or triple by the time we're done. Later, we'll go over our notes and observations and draw some conclusions about what it all means, but not yet.

UNSEEN WORLD
Opposite: The microcosm in a drop of vaginal swab extract is revealed in this photomicrograph. Intact sperm cells with their distinctive tails are seen among epithelial cells, stained to make their glycogen content apparent.

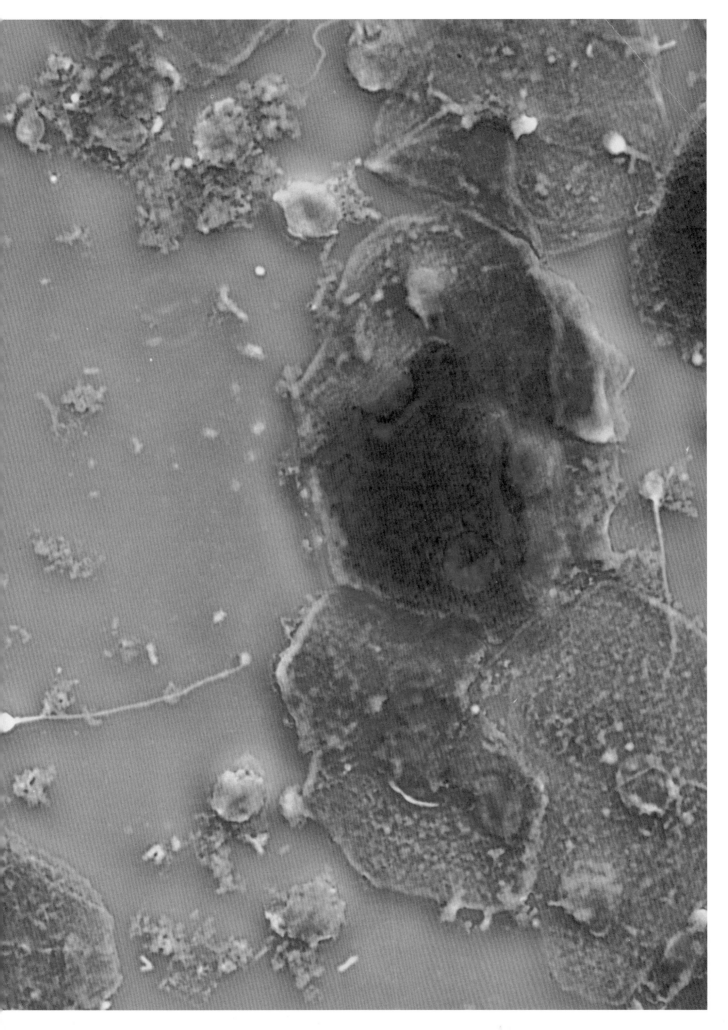

5

Clues in the Dust

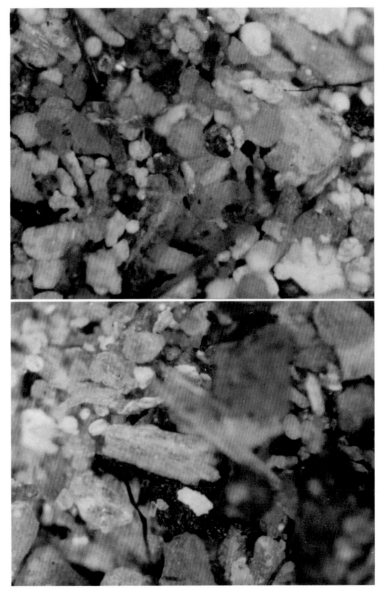

Top: Microscopic debris collected from a rape victim's clothes. *Below:* Similar material was recovered from the suspect's clothes. The similarities between the mixtures include brass chips, paint specks, various minerals and several types of wood.

Going to Disneyland

To enter the miniature world of trace evidence we can't shrink ourselves down, but we can enlarge tiny objects by thousands of times, if necessary. We need to see into places criminals can't even imagine, places where dust and blood burrow, perfectly hidden until uncovered by careful examination.

For the initial examination of the clothing and shoes, our favorite tool is the low power "stereo" microscope. We don't scrimp on quality here, since this stage of the exam will often be the last for many items. If the crime lab pronounces an item clean, it's unlikely anyone will look at that item again. Our low power microscope magnifies between six and forty times actual size and it zooms smoothly throughout the range. The microscope we've chosen has a flexible arm with a bright light attached. It also has a film holder, a kind of permanently attached camera, installed on top. We can select whether to allow light to pass through the lenses to our eyes or up through a system of prisms to the camera. This way we can be sure and photograph exactly what we're seeing.

We're going to settle in for the rest of the day and microscopically examine each and every item of clothing, shoes and tape lifts that were taken from the crime scene and autopsy. The higher the power that is used, the slower the search. As the magnification is increased, the field of view is reduced proportionately. We'll start at six times, 6X, normal size.

After hours of searching evidence under the scope we can almost picture ourselves wandering among clumps of dirt and dust, tiny grains of sand and specks of paint now appearing as huge as boulders. This world is a remarkable place, nicknamed "Disneyland" by one criminalist. We don't know what we're looking for, but we'll know it when we see it. Actually, if we've been to the crime scene, we have a good idea of what is normally going to be found, and we look for something that doesn't belong.

The carpet in Richard and Lisa's home was brown, and there's plenty of proof on the tape lifts. Here and there we spot a few fibers of a teal color that could be from another carpet and we pick them out and save them. Maybe they came from a car, maybe from the bathroom rug, we'll figure it out later if necessary. Both Richard and Lisa are blond, Ralph is dark haired. When we spot a dark brown hair, we'll save it too. We'll even save some of the brown carpet fibers to compare to the actual carpet area next to Richard's body.

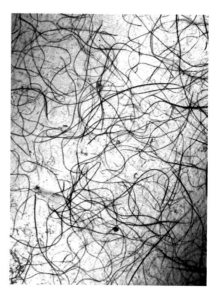

WORLD IN MINIATURE
Stuck to a section of this tape lift are all of the dust and hairs recovered when the tape was rolled over a sofa cushion at a crime scene. The adhesive is not very strong and even the most delicate fibers can be gently pulled off.

No special tools are needed for this phase of the exam. Picking really tiny objects only a few hundredths of an inch long requires a steady hand. Criminalists with nerves of steel can pick out items even smaller. We use tweezers that are similar to those in a medicine cabinet with one important difference—they come to a needle-sharp point enabling us to pluck minuscule objects from the tape.

Trust

Much of what a criminalist deems significant depends on the facts in the case. Here's where it is important that we actually went to the crime scene or are given as much information about the whole case as possible. It doesn't pay for the detectives to keep the criminalist in the dark since we are responsible for sifting through mounds of evidence and finding objects that don't belong. Some investigators are concerned about confidentiality, especially in cases where a suspect has been identified but not yet arrested. There has to be a trusting relationship between criminalist and investigator. It's important for the criminalist not to give off-the-cuff remarks about what he *thinks* the analysis might show, as his credibility will suffer if he's wrong. There are few things more embarrassing than having to go back to a detective and explain why your first impression was dead wrong. Equally important is the free flow of information from the investigator to the criminalist.

Once, an investigator came to us with a rather strange request. He wanted a copy of a blank lab report. When asked why, he sheepishly muttered he was interrogating a suspect, and he was going to show the guy a faked lab report that "proved" evidence found at the scene matched the suspect. Rather than giving the investigator a blank report, we gave him the bum's rush out the door. The damage to the lab's credibility would simply have been irreparable.

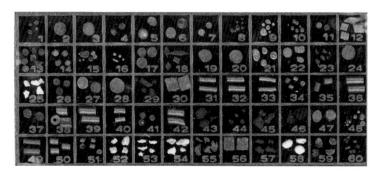

GUNPOWDER PARTICLES come in all shapes and sizes, several of which are shown at right. Many of the long, cylindrical shapes are hollow to promote more efficient burning (see number 38). Each square is one-eighth of an inch.

Tape lifts

The tape lifts collected at the scene are now examined. Each one is actually a piece of cream-colored masking tape about four by five inches in size. The sheets are rolled up sticky side out on a plastic roller marketed as a lint remover for clothing. They are perfect for removing small items from floors, car seats, bodies—any surface. After the tape is exhausted and cannot contain any more evidence, we spread it flat against a square of clear plastic. This allows us to examine what the tape picked up without disturbing it.

Remember the old vacuum salesman's trick of pouring dirt on the floor and asking the prospective customer to "use your old vacuum to clean it up, then use ours?" The same principle works here. Of course, the second vacuuming will reveal considerable dirt left behind by the first. Just once, we'd like to see the customer say, "Just a minute, let's go over the area a third time using my vacuum again and see what *yours* left behind." The law of diminishing returns applies. No method gets everything the first, or even second time. That's also true with the tape lifts. These only take the topmost, or most recent and relevant, layer of dirt and dust from the area on which they're applied. Vacuum cleaners were replaced by tape lifts because we found that vacuums picked up too much debris from deep down, things deposited long before a crime was committed. It also became quite difficult to clean the devices adequately to avoid contamination the next time they were used.

The carpet

The tape taken from the carpet near Richard's body tells us there's a pet in the house. There are black animal hairs that could be from either a cat or a dog. The differences between cat and dog hairs are subtle and distinguishing between them can be challenging. A few hairs are set aside to examine later. Human hairs are easy to pick out, they rarely come to a point or "natural" tip. Present on this tape are many types of human hairs from all parts of the body: head, limb, pubic, beard. Each hair gives information about the source. The tips of the hairs could be razor-cut, broken, crushed, worn, split or natural (pointed). We might look briefly at the roots to see if they were pulled out by force or simply fell out, but we'll save them for future examination. Most of the chores at hand involve picking out and filing samples away for more detailed testing using other equipment.

We notice several white, crystalline particles from one of the tapes taken from the body itself, and we carefully pick them off the adhesive with a needle. Holding our breath, we transfer them to a glass slide and protect them with a coverslip, a thin square of glass which fits over the microscope slide. Several brown human head hairs are removed carefully and "mounted" on another slide. This involves measuring the length of the hair first, then carefully placing the hair into a sticky substance called Permount which will harden with time and allow the hair to be viewed under a microscope more easily. A few greenish plant fragments no bigger than a pencil point are gathered up and saved as well.

Lisa's Clothes

There are no blood stains on any of Lisa's clothes, so we proceed to MUP mapping and search for semen stains. The results are negative indicating that the suspect may have worn a condom during the assault, or perhaps didn't ejaculate at all. Her robe, underwear and bra were also submitted for examination.

On the sticky tapes from Lisa's robe are tiny chips of glass, sparkly and easy to spot. These are collected and placed on a slide. Chips of glass are commonly found in our everyday environment, so we'll need a procedure that can distinguish any glass found associated with the crime scene from "innocent" glass.

Richard's clothing

Next, we turn our attention to Richard's clothing, his shirt, undershirt, pants, shorts, socks and shoes. He died at the scene and his clothing was collected at autopsy. When victims die at the hospital, their blood soaked clothing is considered hazardous, and often placed into sealed plastic bags. It will only take a few hours at room temperature for bacteria to attack the blood, reducing it into a smelly, useless mess. If the clothes are dried first, the decay process is halted. We always wear gloves when we handle any bloody evidence, but fortunately few disease-causing bacteria or viruses can live for more than a few days when dried out.

Richard's shirt is spread out on an examination table. The bloodstains are apparent and lead our eye directly to large spatters raining downward across the chest. The shirt has been hacked apart by paramedics and the cloth is stiff with dried blood. We fit the cut edges back together and staple the shirt back into its original shape. Now we can see the full blood-stain pattern left by the attack.

We'll compare the locations of the wounds on the body with the stains on the clothing. This gives us information about how the clothes were worn when the wounds were inflicted. It may become important later to find that the shirt was flapping open—maybe Richard displayed a gun in his waistband. We can line up the soaking stains in the undershirt and shirt to orient the clothes correctly. The flow of blood may become important in determining whether the body was moved after the wounds were made. Blood always flows to the lowest point, and streams of blood flowing in an upward direction when the was lying faceup could indicate some alteration of the body before the police arrived. We exercise caution before offering such opinions, however, since the medical examiner's act of placing the body into a bag could drastically affect the bloodstains. This is yet another reason to have a criminalist present at the scene.

The direction of the spatters on the shirt and pants gives us an idea of Richard's position while he was being beaten. We see from the autopsy report that there was only one area of the head receiving the blows and there was no other bruising or damage except on his left hand. There was considerable breaking and tearing of scalp and hair, so if the detectives recover an assortment of possible weapons after searching Ralph's car or home, we can apply what we've learned here in selecting the one likely used before performing more detailed and specific testing.

We are always amazed at the trace evidence recovered at an autopsy, and equally appalled at evidence which is overlooked. In this case, the detective with a sharp eye spotted blue flecks on what should have been dull-white skull bone. In another homicide we worked, a tiny chip of brown glass no larger than a couple of pin heads was recovered from the mouth of the victim. Later, a defendant admitted that he and his partner had broken a beer bottle in the victim's mouth before killing him. These cases might not turn on the physical evidence alone but the crime lab proves its value over and over by corroborating or refuting a defendant's story or a prosecutor's theory.

Of course, important evidence can also be overlooked. In a previous homicide case where a blond Caucasian woman had allegedly been raped and beaten to death by a black man, we examined photos taken at her autopsy. Clearly visible on her buttock was a tightly curled black hair.

Both she and her husband were blond. Naturally, we wanted to examine that hair right away. It couldn't be found in any of the packaged evidence sent over from the morgue. It had never been collected. There it was, so tantalizingly close in the photograph yet unavailable for examination under the microscope. No other hairs like it were recovered from the victim's body but a few were found on her clothing.

In another sack we find Richard's shoes. They are both frozen stiff. We'll let them thaw out for an hour or so. Everything which might have biological evidence on it must be stored in the freezer. The freezers in the property room are enormous in order to keep all of the evidence from rapes and homicides over the years. Evidence cannot be discarded until a case has been completely concluded, including appeals.

The right shoe is fairly clean and free of anything which looks like blood. Several suspicious looking stains on the soles are tested, but with negative results. The left side of the left shoe has a fine cream-colored powder on it, sort of a light yellow. We'll carefully remove as much as we can and save it for chemical analysis. There are a few small spatters which test positive for blood near the toe.

To minimize the potential for contamination, we'll wait until we've finished examining the victim's clothing and clean up thoroughly before looking at Ralph's clothing. We'll change gloves between items of evidence and change our white lab coat before opening evidence from a different person.

Ralph's clothes

The clothes taken from Ralph are packaged together with his shoes. This is unfortunate since now any trace evidence such as fibers or dust which was only on one of the items could rub onto the other items. We will include a word about this next time we give a training session to the police agency responsible for collecting these items. Each item should have been packaged separately. The good news is that blood dries quickly, so the bloodstains on the shoes didn't transfer to anything else.

No blood spatters are seen on Ralph's pants or shirt. If he committed the crime, we think he was probably wearing different clothing. Given the amount of blood spattering at the scene, the assailant should have had considerable blood on his clothing. If Ralph was the attacker and these are not the clothes he wore, there is little to be gained by searching further.

His shoes, on the other hand, are a mess of soiled stains. Some of the stains are oily, some have a distinct directionality to them, leading from the toe towards the heel. The shoes aren't as bloody as we would expect, but if the attacker had been standing to the victim's right, the victim's legs and feet could have shadowed most of the blood from getting on the attacker's shoes. Interestingly, no glass fragments are seen in the upper surfaces and seams of these shoes but we will be sampling those directional stains and testing for blood.

During our examination of Ralph's shoes under the low power microscope, we notice again a cream or light yellow powder lying just on the surface of some of the spatters. It looks interesting, and some of the powder is collected for analysis using instruments and methods described in the next chapter.

Picking and sorting, saving for later. That's the routine we follow for the rest of the day. We'll be organizing dozens of bits of evidence too small to be noticed by a criminal in a big hurry.

6

Tools of the Trade

The initial examination of evidence often begins under the low power stereo microscope. The dark ring in the middle part of the microscope's body is marked off with magnification factors that can be increased or decreased.

SEPARATIONS

The physical world is not made up of pure substances; we encounter complex mixtures and compounds every day. Gasoline, food and blood each contain thousands of pure compounds in appropriate proportions all mixed together. What's useful about mixtures is that they can be separated again into their individual components. In the lab we use devices that can do this rapidly and accurately. At least a century ago a scientist discovered that two colored dyes in water would separate when dripped onto absorbent paper. After a drop was placed on paper and allowed to absorb, one could see that the different dyes absorbed into the paper at different rates. Instead of a single spot of dye, there would be a spot with two rings, each of a different color.

So began the science of chromatography, literally to "write with color." As the technique evolved other substances besides paper were used, proving more effective. Now, hollow tubes full of special chemicals take the place of the paper and a gentle flow of nitrogen or helium gas propels the heated, vaporized mixture along the length of it. At the end of this tube, or column as it is named, is a sensitive detector, nowadays hooked to a computer, of course. This is the gas chromatograph, or GC, for short.

The whole point is to take an unknown mixture and separate it into its various components. When examining a blood sample we want to identify any alcohol or drugs along with the other normal components. If the sample is from debris recovered after a fire, we can look for traces of gasoline or the residue of some other ignitable liquid. Crime labs have gradually built vast libraries of standard compounds to compare to evidence samples. These will be used to identify poisons, explosives, drugs, volatile fuels, plastics and anything else that can be dissolved and sent through the GC.

The race is to the swift

To understand how the GC works imagine a line of eager racehorses all waiting at the gate. Each horse signifies a pure substance and all of them together represents the mixture. They all begin the race at the same time. This is similar to what happens in the GC. A small amount, maybe as much as a pinhead, of unknown material is dissolved in a solvent such as alcohol and injected with a precision needle into the GC. The flag goes up and they're off. After a short time something begins to happen. Horses run at different speeds. They may all start at the same place, but as they run along the track the group spreads out according to each horse's natural speed. It's the same with chemicals in the GC. Temperature, gas flow and the chemical's own properties influence the individual components of the mixture. What we get at the other end, the detector, are substances crossing the finish line at different times. What started out as a mixture ends up as a series of pure, separated compounds coming out one at a time. The detector senses these substances and records their presence on a chart or graph. As each chemical emerges from the column a pen plots a line, rising in proportion to the amount of the chemical present. If no chemical is present the pen draws only a flat line. An electronic timer checks to see how long it takes each chemical to travel the length of the column. After all of the components have emerged, the pen returns to a flat baseline, ready for the next analysis. The resulting chart is made up of peaks and valleys showing a profile of what's in the original mixture.

Modern GC's are extremely sensitive and can detect some substances down to several billionths of a gram or less. It's still up to the criminalist to determine what the pure components are. All the GC can do is suggest what they might be and how many there are. We run known pure samples routinely to see how much time they take to pass through the GC, then we compare the results to an unknown chemical that comes out at exactly the same time.

WORKHORSE OF THE CRIME LAB, gas chromatographs are used in the detection of small traces of chemicals and separating complex mixtures. Fire debris, toxicology and even blood alcohol determinations are made with this device. The one pictured at right is in operation in a large crime laboratory in the Republic of Ireland. To the left of the GC is a bottle of compressed helium, a gas used to carry the vaporized sample through the instrument.

Burning questions

The examination of the fire debris samples from the burned and unburned areas of the living room is next. The samples are each stored in airtight, quart-sized metal cans with friction lids similar to paint cans. This prevents substances from evaporating. It's extremely important to package fire debris evidence this way. We worked a case once where the police department submitted several pieces of burned wood recovered from a suspicious fire in a bar. They had carefully packaged the wood in paper sacks, just like we train them to do—for blood evidence! Two months later they asked us to check the wood for traces of gasoline. The tests all came up negative. Small wonder.

Our evidence cans will be warmed up in a laboratory oven set to a little less than 212 degrees Fahrenheit, the boiling point of water. We don't want to heat the cans to the point where the lids pop off, but we have to warm up the evidence in case there are oily substances like diesel fuels that cannot be detected at cooler temperatures.

The method we use for detecting ignitable liquids is quite clever. It was borrowed from the air pollution scientists and perfected by a chemist at the Bureau of Alcohol, Tobacco and Firearms. The original scientists discovered that a strip of Teflon, coated with activated charcoal, trap vapors at very low concentrations and hold them there. Prior to analysis, the trapped vapors could be washed off with a laboratory solvent and injected into the gas chromatograph. Criminalists liked the idea, so we adopted it for fire debris analysis in crime labs around the world.

The essence of fire debris, or arson, analysis is to assist the arson investigator to determine the cause and origin of a fire. If a criminal uses a substance to speed up, or accelerate a fire, traces may remain after the fire is extinguished. When gasoline, for example, is poured onto a wooden floor some of the liquid seeps down into the crevices between the boards and never gets enough oxygen to burn. Traces of solvents can often withstand otherwise devastating fires.

At Richard and Lisa's home the sofa, next to Richard's body, and the carpeted floor next to the sofa had started to burn. On the floor there was a clear, well-defined area of melted carpet in a "halo" pattern. A liquid had been poured on the floor and then set ablaze. Fortunately, neither the carpet nor the sofa fire grew out of control. In fact, the ceiling didn't reveal any soot damage.

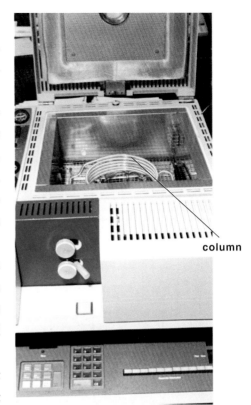

column

THE OVEN LID on the gas chromatograph is lifted up to reveal the column, a coiled hollow glass tube. Just underneath the column is another, much thinner, tube called a capillary column, used for precise analysis and separating even more complex mixtures. *Below:* A precision needle used to inject the sample into the GC.

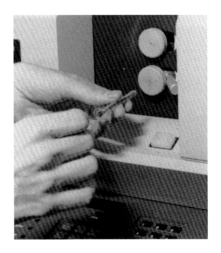

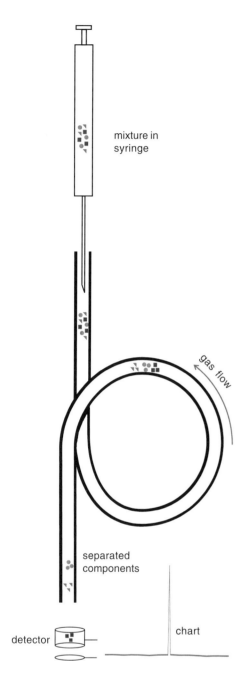

mixture in syringe

gas flow

separated components

detector

chart

RELYING ON CHEMICAL DIFFERENCES such as boiling point, the gas chromatograph separates out components of a mixture. The mixture under test is injected into a coiled column (*top*), the individual components emerging later to be picked up by a sensitive electronic detector which registers a peak on the chart (*bottom*).

To analyze this evidence we pry open the can with the burned carpet sample. We do this under a fume hood, a chamber with an exhaust fan similar to the one on top of a kitchen range. This removes any hazardous vapors that might otherwise escape into the lab. We look quickly, since vapors that might have formed over our carpet sample might escape and it's those very vapors we want to analyze. Visually inspecting the contents of the can is necessary because we wouldn't want to put a can with liquid gasoline or something equally dangerous into a warm oven. In our present case that may not be a problem, but it's a good habit since we often receive evidence that other people have collected.

When we catch a whiff of the vapor, it reminds us of something volatile, but we can't recognize it. We like to sniff the air above the can by gently wafting the fumes towards us even though we may be exposed to dangerous chemicals. If the can had been collected at the scene of a chemical factory fire we probably wouldn't use this method of observation, but ordinarily our sense of smell is one of our tools. We jokingly call it an "olfactory chromatogram." Our nose isn't nearly as sensitive as a hound, but we can identify some common solvents, paint and nail polish removers to name a few. In this case, the smell is just too faint to be sure.

While we have the lid off, we place a short strip of the charcoal-coated plastic dangling by a string into the can, just above the evidence. When we replace the lid, the string is held in place by the friction and pressure of the lid against the can. The strip dangles in the can collecting a variety of vapors until we're ready to analyze it. If necessary, two sets of charcoal strips may be left in the cans, one remaining overnight, to try and gather even more fumes. We know the detectives recovered a bottle of rubbing alcohol from the kitchen, but we won't jump to any conclusions.

Each of the cans is prepared the same way. The comparison samples should come out clean, and the burned samples should show what was poured on them. At least that's the way we hope it will go. Burned carpet is notorious for releasing complex by-products called pyrolysis (pie-ROL-isis) products that can be confused with accelerants. Because of this, we proceed with due care. If we need to, we can always burn some of the comparison carpet sample to see what substances it produces when there are no accelerants. We must always be ready to do a little "research project" like that to answer questions that arise during our examination.

After the cans have warmed in the oven for several hours, we remove them and let them cool. The charcoal strips are removed, one by one, and placed into a little glass vial. We add a drop or two of a purified solvent called carbon disulfide. This dissolves almost any solvent we're likely to encounter in casework but itself isn't likely to be used by an arsonist. Carbon disulfide goes through the gas chromatograph first so it won't be confused with any other compounds which might be there.

The graph from the GC is flat, which indicates there is nothing other than the solvent we added here in the lab. That's good, since we are running our comparison samples first. The comparison samples are unburned sections of carpet and sofa cut near the burned and melted areas. This helps us rule out glues and adhesives, carpet and upholstery cleaners or other compounds which might have been present, but not involved in the fire. If we had rushed the job and analyzed the burned samples first,

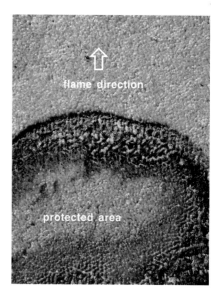

HALO PATTERN
When flammable liquids are ignited on synthetic carpeting they can produce burn patterns similar to the one pictured (*above*). As the liquid burns, an area of damage extends outward from the edge of the burning liquid (in this case rubbing alcohol). The evaporating liquid actually cools the surface of the carpet directly under the liquid resulting in the undamaged center of the pattern.

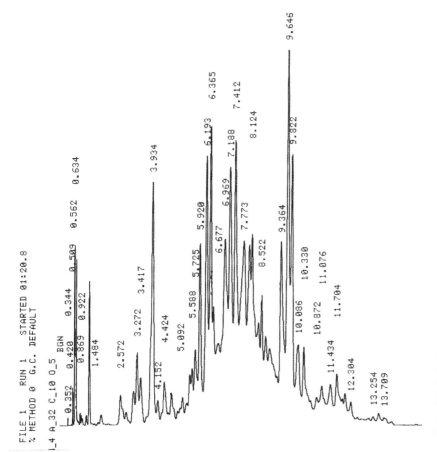

PEAKS AND VALLEYS on this GC chart reveal the components of a sample of burned carpet. Each sharp peak represents a separate compound. The size of the peak is proportional to how much material is present. The numbers above each peak give the exact time in minutes it took that compound to travel through the column from the moment of injection to its detection.

we might have seen a result suggestive of an accelerant, but was actually just a glue residue from the carpet backing. Having establish clean comparison samples, we can now run the burned samples.

The GC results from the burned area of the carpet show a typical pattern of compounds often found when plastic, especially carpet, burns. This pattern has been mistaken for gasoline by careless examiners, but with excellent training we immediately see it for what it is, a negative result. The sofa is made of cotton fabric, probably treated to retard fire. Its GC printout also shows nothing suggestive of any ignitable liquid. If an accelerant was used, it may have been in extremely tiny amounts, or could have been something like the rubbing alcohol which simply evaporated by the time we collected the samples.

What we have shown is the absence of evidence. Someone once said the absence of evidence is not the evidence of absence. We have neither confirmed nor ruled out that the rubbing alcohol was used to start the fire. We may be asked to speculate in court as to whether we would have expected to find a residue of gasoline, for example, if it had been used. In such a brief and contained fire, there probably would have been some detectable residue of a "heavier" compound. Heavier compounds include gasoline or kerosine. Our experience tells us that these compounds were probably not used to start this fire, but we have only a little information about what was actually used. The fire was started by something liquid, and volatile enough to be gone completely by the time we collected our samples. This might suggest something like acetone or alcohol.

Over the rainbow

When we're trying to identify an unknown substance we need to gather as much information about it as possible. If we have enough sample we may burn it, smell it or crush it with tweezers under the microscope. All of these tests reveal something about its physical properties, but what we need to do is to determine its molecular makeup. One way to do this is with the science of spectroscopy.

It may have been Sir Isaac Newton who discovered that white light was really made up of all colors mixed together. When light passes through a glass prism or raindrop a beautiful rainbow appears. Later, scientists found that each color of light was really a separate entity. Different energy levels created different colors. Moving from low to high energy we

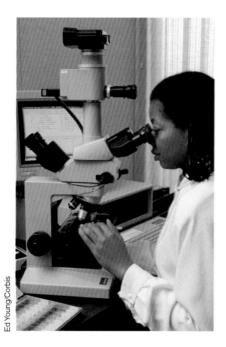

Ed Young/Corbis

A SPECIALIZED CAMERA is mounted on the top of the microscope to capture and record the criminalist's observations. Objective lenses mounted on a turret (near the operator's left hand) may be rotated into place to give the desired magnification.

get red, orange, yellow, green, blue and violet. As the science of physics matured, special instruments were made that to sense "colors" the human eye couldn't detect. These colors, the reddest red and the deepest violet, extended beyond the rainbow.

Redder than red

When an electric stove element heats up, just before it glows red, we can feel its heat. We can sense heat with our skin. We are feeling infrared, literally "below red," energy. Our eyes can't see this "light," but some special films can take a picture using this heat as their only source of illumination. If we turn up the energy, the element glows cherry red. We have now increased the energy to the point where our eyes can see this light. Scientists have found that many molecules absorb infrared or "IR" energy. The bonds between their atoms react to IR by rocking, shaking and bending in predictable ways. We use a sensitive instrument called the infrared spectrometer that focuses IR energy on a sample and records the sample's ability to absorb the energy.

Just as in the GC, a graph records peaks and valleys. The movement of the line is proportional to the amount of energy absorbed by the molecules of the chemicals. Thousands of chemicals have been analyzed, their graphs recorded and published. Now we can run our unknown chemical and compare its IR chart to known chemicals, hopefully finding a match. The charts are so detailed that when a chart from an unknown chemical exactly matches the chart of a known chemical, we can be sure to have identified it. This is one of the few times in the crime lab when we can positively identify a specific unknown substance.

Most of our tests give us hints about the nature of the unknown, but only a few tests can positively identify something. There's always a drawback, however, and the IR is no exception. The chemicals placed in the IR for analysis must be clean and pure. The IR is not a separation device like the GC. We must spend some time cleaning up our unknown chemically before placing it into this machine. This usually means extracting it with solvents to remove unwanted companion chemicals. A sign posted on a crime lab wall summed it up this way:

"Analysis of dirty samples is half-fast."

The infrared charts of the paint samples from our case are unmistakable. In looking at the overall shape of the lines from each chart we see that where one goes up, they all go up and vice versa. The two charts will never be exact duplicates of each other; if they were we might suspect something amiss. The peaks and valleys all line up, however, and there is an IR match between the paints. The colors matched under the microscope, too, and thus another part of the puzzle falls into place.

Paint is a mixture of at least two components, pigment and vehicle. The color is determined by the pigment, small, highly-colored particles of chemicals suspended in a plastic base called the vehicle. The mixture is dissolved in a solvent that slowly evaporates away leaving the colorful pigment embedded in a plastic film. The approach to comparing our two samples of paint, one from the crowbar and one from the skull, will take into consideration the color, texture, presence or absence of layers, the trace elements present and results of IR testing.

The chips were too small to simply place into the instrument so we had to use a little more sophisticated technology. The two chips will be compared using the IR microscope. This instrument is a marriage of a

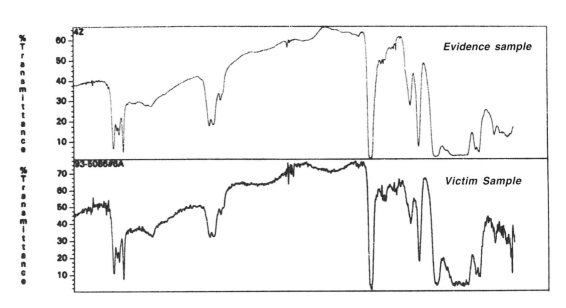

PAINT COMPARED by infrared spectrometry can show numerous similarities or differences. In the top graph a sample of evidence paint is compared to the lower graph, a speck of paint from the victim. Each peak and valley of the graph indicates the sample's ability to pass infrared energy. The deeper the valley, the less energy is able to penetrate the sample.

microscope with an IR spectrometer. It allows us to focus IR energy onto a very small area. We use the microscope as a precise aiming device and let the instrument take its readings.

The IR microscope is much like our other microscopes with one important difference: There aren't any lenses to pass the IR energy. Since IR is heat and glass absorbs heat, the energy would be blocked from getting to the sample. The optics in the IR part of the device are really mirrors. When focusing on the sample, we're looking through plain glass optics, but then these are swung out of the way and a system of curved mirrors is lined up over the sample. Infrared energy is passed from the instrument through the scope and into the sample. Another set of mirrors returns what energy remains back to the sensitive detectors inside the instrument. The whole thing is incredibly quick, taking just a minute or so. The device uses a branch of mathematics called Fourier (FOR-ee-ay) transform to calculate the sample's absorption of a whole range of energy levels. The formal name of the instrument is FT-IR or Fourier Transform InfraRed.

After the IR test, we see that the IR charts are virtually identical between the two chips. This tells us that the plastic vehicle of the paints are the same. We still can't call it a match because there's more to paint than the vehicle. There are additional tests we could do, actually burning the chips in a device called a pyroprobe (PIE-ro-probe). This device burns a fleck of paint in a flash and feeds the resulting vapor into a gas chromatograph. The graph or chart from this test shows numerous peaks and valleys corresponding to the breaking down of the plastic under high temperature. This test is obviously destructive and we don't do it unless it can give us more information than we already have. Our chips only have a single layer of paint, but in the case of multiple paint layers, the IR may give misleading results and we would need to do a pyroprobe test. We'll probably never be able to say that the paint on the skull could *only* have come from the paint on that one single crowbar but we'll settle for the phrase "chemically indistinguishable."

Bluer than blue

In many ways, the ultraviolet spectrum is similar to the infrared. The difference is that the energy is much higher, now we're off the visible scale at the blue or violet end. Again, our eyes can't see this light but we know it's there because of the way molecules react when subjected to it. Parts of the atoms making up a molecule, called electrons, get excited, soaking up ultraviolet (UV) energy. We have an instrument called the UV spectrophotometer (spek-tro-fo-TOM-eh-ter) that features a sensitive detector able to pick up this absorption. A chart in some ways similar to the IR spectrometer is produced, having peaks proportional to the amount of UV absorbed. Not all molecules respond to UV but most drugs do. Even though it's not as specific as the IR, this test gives additional information about unknown chemicals allowing us to fit more pieces of the identification puzzle together. Once again, libraries of known chemicals have been subjected to UV energy and their charts recorded and published. We don't use this test for paint, but it will come in handy for things like drug analysis. The results are searched for a good match between what's been published before and a chemical under scrutiny.

By now the reader may have imagined connecting the output of a separation device such as the GC to a sensitive and specific detector such as the IR. This is a good idea, although expensive. Some of our best equipment comes from a marriage of selectivity and specificity.

Inventions

During the 1984 Olympics officials needed a way to identify substances called anabolic steroids that might be present in the bodies of athletes. These steroids are naturally present in humans at very low levels.

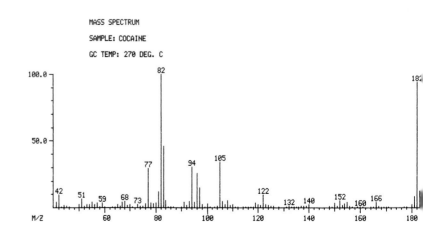

SHATTERED MOLECULES of cocaine hydrochloride register as thin lines on the gas chromatograph/mass spectrometer. The instrument directs a beam of electrons on the sample, breaking the molecule apart. The numbers indicate the mass of each resulting fragment, the height of the line is related to their abundance.

When taken as supplements, they have the potential to dramatically increase muscle mass. Merely showing the presence of steroids was not enough to disqualify an athlete, one needed to quantitate, or show how much steroid was present. Steroids are very complex molecules and are not easy to analyze. Furthermore, blood is full of proteins and sugars at high levels, compared to tiny amounts of steroids that might be present.

Enter, the 'black box'

An instrument known as a GC/MS (gas chromatograph/mass spectrometer) was used to solve the dilemma. Until recently, this sensitive instrument was not in many crime labs. They used to be extremely expensive and required lots of high-tech maintenance. The older models filled up entire rooms, now they sit on table tops. How they operate is a study in ingenuity: The front end is really a GC exactly like the one we described above. The difference is in the detector, called a mass spectrometer. What we have in the GC/MS is not a passive detector that simply records the amount of some unnamed compound as it traverses the tube; this detector actually rips the molecule apart and examines its fragments in detail.

Molecules can be represented by a model made up of balls and sticks. A ball represents an atom and a stick represents a bond that joins atoms together. The strength of a bond, or "glue," holding atoms together depends on which type of atoms are connected, but that strength is pre-

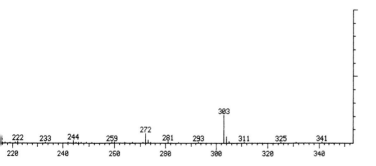

dictable. A steroid molecule, for example, contains atoms of carbon, hydrogen and oxygen all connected together by bonds. The strength of the bonds joining oxygen to carbon is different than those joining carbon to hydrogen, but it is predictable that all molecules of steroid will behave the same way. The GC/MS fires electron "bullets" at the steroid molecules until some of the bonds break. Not all of the bonds break, just certain weak ones; the others are left intact. The molecules fragment in the same way each time. The resulting fragments shoot down a tube until they are detected by a sensitive detector hooked up to a computer. The heaviest fragments are the ones with the most mass, that's the "mass" in mass spectrometer. These are separated out from the lightest ones. It's all quite orderly and repeatable.

The computer recognizes the fragments and assigns them each a mass value according to the sum total of the atoms present (two carbons, three hydrogens, for example). The mass values are compared to a huge library of compounds that have been previously run by other labs. Some of these libraries have tens of thousands of compounds in them. The computer finds as close a match as it can and prints out a list of possible substances.

The GC/MS is also considered to be specific. An excellent match between reference data and an unknown is conclusive. Where we have to be careful is when the "matches" are less than perfect. A serious problem occurs when the instruments used in crime labs are thought of as "black boxes." When the criminalist doesn't understand how the devices function or what its limitations are, incorrect conclusions might be drawn.

"Put the sample in one end and get the answer out the other."

You'd better believe it

When beginning math students are first taught how to use a calculator, they may be given a problem such as "eleven into three." They'll invariably type eleven, press the divide by key and then enter the number three. They get 3.6666 and record the answer. It must be right because the answer is displayed on the calculator. What the students lack is the experience and self-confidence that would enable them to disbelieve their device and check the answer for reasonableness. The same mentality can be found among some criminalists. There's an old story about a criminalist on the witness stand telling the jury about two samples of paint. The two samples were analyzed with the finest, most expensive instruments in the lab and matched perfectly. What he'd failed to note was that one sample was red the other blue. We call it the black box mentality and it's something to resist always and everywhere in our profession. Another glaring example occurred in a fairly famous trial.

Leading astray

A tube filled with blood, drawn from a person's arm, will clot and soon spoil. For this reason a chemical preservative and anticoagulant is added to the tube before any blood is drawn. These chemicals mix with the blood to prevent clotting and inhibit bacteria from growing. A common chemical used for this purpose is called EDTA (ethylenediamine-tetraacetate).

At one point in the O.J. Simpson murder trial, defense lawyers made allegations that the police had dripped blood from a collection tube onto a gate at the crime scene. The claim was made that this blood could not have come from a wounded person. The prosecution attempted to refute this by demonstrating that there was no preservative (EDTA) present in the bloodstain, and that there should have been if the blood came out of a collection tube. Samples of the blood from the tube and the stain in question were sent to a federal crime laboratory. A chemist analyzed the samples even using his own blood as a reference sample at one point. This chemist may have been very good at his job in the lab, but it is our firm opinion that he led the jury astray because of the black box mentality.

When he testified in court, the government chemist showed at least two charts, similar in principle to those depicted here. The court display he used showed a GC/MS graph of an analysis of blood from the collection tube and one from a sample of blood found on the gate. Like a home stereo, the GC/MS has a powerful amplifier in it to boost faint signals. And, like the home stereo, when the gain is cranked up the amplifier boosts noise right along with the signal resulting in a noisy background. If there is a loud signal, there's no problem. His display clearly showed a high peak indicating EDTA in the control sample. When we described the GC, we mentioned how the size of the peak is directly proportional to the amount of substance the instrument is detecting. There's a lot of EDTA in that sample, as we would expect. The scale on the left side of each graph tells how hard the amplifier is working. It's labeled in multiples of ten. This is most important. The computer can be set to determine the appropriate scale on the left side of the chart. This is called the "autoscale" feature. The computer tries to find the highest peak on the chart and adjust the scale on the left so that the tallest peak reaches just to the top of the page, or full scale. Ordinarily, this is useful since it prevents a strong peak from going off the chart, making us rerun the graph.

The next chart this chemist showed was the one that caused all the trouble. Jagged lines indicating a noisy background were displayed but magnified in the extreme. The computer couldn't find a good, tall peak so it kept increasing the gain or amplification of the chart until something fit. The scale on the left side of this graph shows that the multiples of ten have greatly reduced in value. There was no EDTA, but the computer dutifully "turned up the volume" so high looking for a signal that the background noise went to nearly full scale. Asking a jury to look at the two charts as if they were comparable is unfair. It's hard enough for trained criminalists to interpret two charts printed at different scales. Was there a lab policy preventing the government chemist from replotting the two

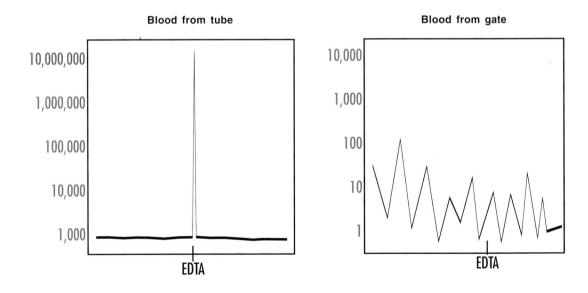

SCALING FACTORS INFLUENCE the way data is interpreted. The left graph shows a clear, strong signal indicating the presence of EDTA, a substance added to blood collection tubes. If plotted on a similar scale, the graph on the right would be virtually flat.

charts at the same scale? If he had, the second chart would have been as flat as a pancake, no EDTA, no question.

It gets better. The defense hired their own "scientist" who only looked at the government's printouts. He never did a single experiment on his own. He must have been delighted when he saw the two charts, for there, among the noise peaks and valleys was a little bump corresponding to EDTA. *Hey! There it is, see? They must have planted the blood!* Sure, and there were also bumps corresponding to every compound on the planet detectable by this equipment. Was the finding meaningful? Did either expert's testimony assist the jury in reaching a just conclusion?

It may seem a small point, and in this trial, it probably was. Good science and unambiguous testimony probably would not have changed the outcome. Does that mean the next trial will be so forgiving? We think not and strive to keep our standards high.

Now that we have a basic understanding of how a few of the more prominent crime lab instruments work, let's see how they are used in casework.

7

Trace Evidence

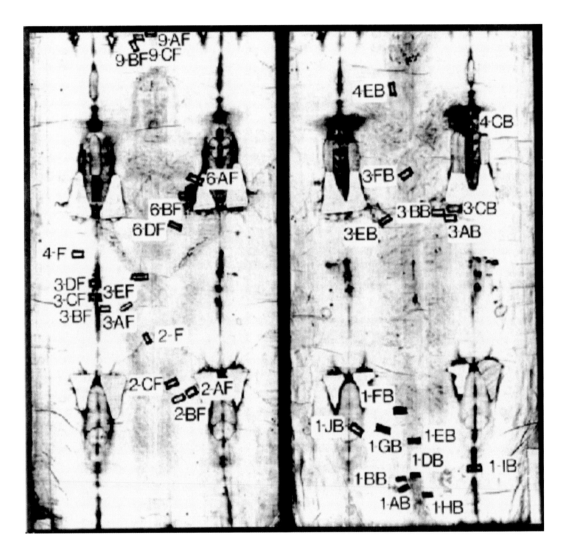

One of the most well known trace evidence cases in the world involved the examination of the shroud of Turin by scientists hoping to determine its actual age. The cloth of the shroud was eventually dated at 14th century and the "bloodstains" identified by microscopy as early paint pigments. The numbered marks indicate areas sampled with tape lifts.

HAIRS AND FIBERS

An eighty-nine year-old woman was alone in her home when a man in his thirties broke in through an unlocked sliding glass door. He bound the woman tightly with telephone and extension cord, and she was unable to break free. For a whole day, she was unable to get food or water. By the time she was discovered, her hands had become gangrenous and required amputation. The district attorney asked us to check the ends of the wire used to bind her and see if a knife had been used. The use of a knife during the commission of this type of crime could bring a more harsh prison sentence. At first it looked like the wires had been cut; the ends were clean and not jagged. Upon microscopic examination we saw that the ends of the copper wires showed a peculiar narrowing, then a separation, rather than a sharp edge which we would expect if the wires had been cut. After trying out various ideas on actual samples of the wires including cutting and pulling, we concluded that the assailant had probably stepped on one end of the wires and pulled sharply upward, snapping the wires in two.

Also, a gray wig hair was discovered on the bed where the victim had been found. The "hair" was actually made of Dynel, a synthetic fiber used in wigs. Immediately we thought we might have found an important clue, perhaps the assailant wore a disguise. We recalled that the woman had a gray wig on her bedroom dresser. After retrieving that wig and comparing its fibers to the evidence microscopically, we decided that the "hair" was probably from her own wig and unrelated to the crime.

As a side note, fiber evidence usually associates, rather than conclusively identifies an individual with a crime scene. Synthetic fibers are generally produced in huge quantities but sometimes a fiber with an unusual cross section or one made from an uncommon plastic is discovered that can link a suspect to a series of crime scenes. A few natural fibers, such as white cotton, are so common it's tempting to ignore them altogether. The colorful dyes used on many fibers add to their distinctiveness. We always look for the combination of fibers associated with the crime scene and those found on a victim or suspect.

The sweet-tooth bandit

In a different and rather bizarre case, two men were stopped by police near a recently burglarized home. On the kitchen counter of this

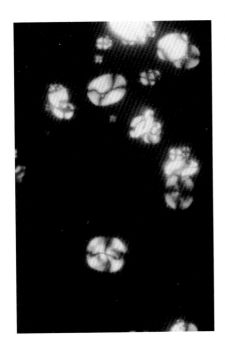

STARCH PARTICLES seen under the polarized light microscope. *Above:* Wheat, *below:* corn. Both samples have been magnified about 375 times. The peculiar Maltese cross appearance is the effect of polarized light on the arrangement of starch molecules in each grain. The crosses appear much darker in the cornstarch. After starch is cooked, the effect disappears.

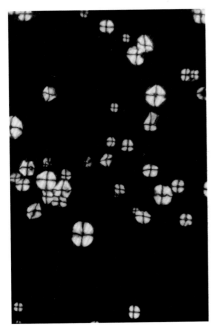

home was a freshly baked chocolate cake, intended for a birthday party later that day. As burglary can be a somewhat strenuous activity, the burglars had apparently gotten hungry and helped themselves to a generous portion. Shortly afterward, two of the men were caught outside near the house with some property belonging to the burglarized home. When one suspect was asked what the dark substance was under his fingernails, he came up with a story about how he'd just finished a chocolate cake dessert from a local fast-food restaurant. Not bad for thinking on his feet. The arresting officer was also pretty quick and pulled out a paper clip, to take a sample from under the suspect's fingernail. He also took samples of the cake in the kitchen and submitted both to the lab.

This case captured the fancy of one of criminalists in the lab. He asked the detective to go out to the restaurant and purchase a chocolate cake dessert of the same type as the alleged burglar said he'd eaten. He microscopically compared the samples of frosting and cake from each of the locations to see if they were different. Some background information was needed. Were the ingredients of the recipe used by the fast-food restaurant ever varied, or could they be considered constant? There is considerable competition among the makers of food for fast-food eateries and a telephone call from the criminalist to the cake manufacturer was not answered. Apparently a phone message from some fellow claiming to be from a local sheriff's crime lab was not enough to pry loose the frosting's "secret" formula. A detective was invited to help out. The officer went so far as to threaten the president of the company with a search warrant. Finally, the company returned the phone call from the lab, offering complete cooperation.

Starch was the key. The two recipes were remarkably similar except that the homemade frosting used a mixture of uncooked corn and wheat starch as a thickener while the commercial frosting used only corn starch. A factory representative verified that they never used wheat starch in the frosting. Under the polarized light microscope the difference was clearly visible. The suspect was lying. The starch in the frosting under his nails was both corn and wheat. Without witnesses or fingerprints, the two were found guilty of burglary in a subsequent jury trial. Of course, the fact that one of the jurors had worked at Betty Crocker for more than twenty years couldn't have hurt much either.

Close-up view

Each of these cases illustrates the use of what could be our most important laboratory instrument besides our own brains—the microscope. Criminals can clean up the scene by moving bodies, wiping up blood or even burning the area, but they have a tough time removing what they can't see. Our greatest power as criminalists lies in being able to see otherwise invisible traces and having the luxury of sufficient time to pursue their identification. The very nature of a criminal act is hurried and frantic, but criminalists can spend day after day sifting through evidence looking for transfers from suspect to crime scene and vice versa.

The compound light microscope is but one of many variations on a theme. Think of it merely as a fancy magnifying lens and an eyepiece. Over the centuries, more and more sophisticated lenses have been ground to correct various optical defects. Modern microscopes use computer-designed lenses to give crisp, sharp, color-corrected images. Some even come with television cameras attached allowing a group of observers to see exactly what we're seeing.

Light microscopes are alike in having a light source in the base, a flat piece called a stage to hold the specimen, an objective lens that does the bulk of the magnification and a hollow tube with an eyepiece for increasing the magnification. A knob on the side raises and lowers the stage to allow focusing of the image. Several objective lenses are mounted on a rotating turret and a variety of magnifications are therefore available by rotating a different lens into place. The objective lens may be a 40X lens, the eyepiece a 10X. In that case, a specimen would be enlarged forty times by the objective and then ten more times by the eyepiece for a total of 400 times. This would make an object only a hundredth of an inch long appear to be four inches long.

We can easily observe transparent objects with this arrangement. Even normally opaque objects such as paint, wood, rocks, plastic, tissue and bone allow light to pass through quite well when they are thinly sliced or chipped. Metal is one of the few things that light can't penetrate and it will appear black. For those kind of specimens, we simply turn on a small, bright light which passes downward from above the sample instead of upwards through the base. A special type of setup called coaxial illumination allows the same tube to send both light going down towards the sample and back up to our eyes. With this illumination setup we can

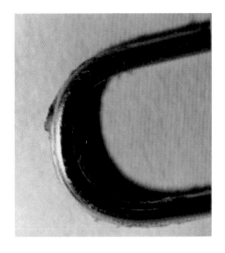

IMPROVISED IN THE FIELD
A paperclip used by a quick-thinking officer to scrape under the fingernail of the equally quick-thinking burglar. Note the traces of fudge frosting and chocolate cake on the edges.

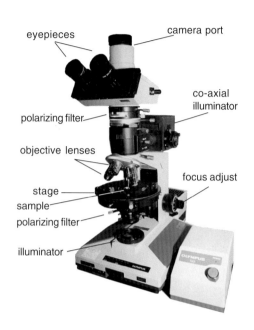

FANCY MAGNIFYING GLASS
Light microscopes are used in crime labs for high power magnification. The circular stage shows that this model is set up for polarized light. The effects of polarized light depend upon the rotation of the sample and filters. The circular stage is marked off in degrees and can be turned accurately.

view the surface of metal and thick objects very clearly at high magnification. This allows us a closer inspection than with the low-power stereo microscope we used to look over the evidence.

The maximum magnification we can achieve with the light microscope is about 1200X. This is powerful enough to see a single bacterium. We rarely need more magnification than this but when we do, we use a scanning electron microscope (SEM). Instead of light waves, the SEM uses an electron beam to illuminate the specimen. Some kinds of trace evidence, such as particles of gunshot residue, must be magnified 5,000 times or more to be identified. In addition to displaying the image of the particles, the SEM reports their elemental composition. The combination of image plus composition gives us valuable clues to identify an unknown particle.

Take another look

Another useful microscope is the polarized light microscope (PLM). This instrument is like the light microscope with one difference. Above and below the specimen are polarizing filters, similar in principle to the ones found in expensive sunglasses. Many types of plastic, minerals and biological materials like starch all look distinctive and acquire various colors under polarized light. We can gain information about the crystal structure of a drug or mineral by using this microscope. Some materials, including glass, have no crystal structure and are easily spotted with this method of illumination. Starch grains look like white dots with little "Maltese crosses" in the center. Nothing else looks quite like these. Synthetic carpet fibers give the appearance of miniature rainbows, displaying a full spectrum of colors along their edges. The hue and intensity of the colors depends upon the kind of plastic in the fibers.

Since microscopy is nondestructive, we can look at the only remaining particle recovered from a crime scene all day long and not disturb it in any way. It will still be available the next day for anyone else to look at. Many of the tests we do are destructive and after those tests are completed, the small amount we used is gone. Microscopy allows many different types of lighting arrangements without harming the evidence.

Even if some microscopical techniques are old it doesn't mean they're ineffective. Light microscopy is used by scientists all over the world to identify fibers, minerals, organisms and complex chemicals including drugs and explosives residue. Some of the world's leading microscopists work at the McCrone Research Institute in Chicago. Founded by Walter C. McCrone in 1956, the MRI has become a center for training new microscopists and offers expert assistance in the identification of microscopic particles to research and industry.

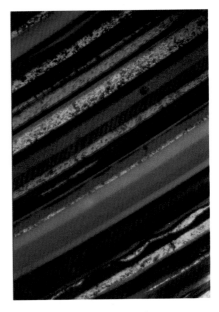

Shrouded in mystery

Dr. McCrone was the lone voice insisting that the microscopic evidence proved the infamous shroud of Turin to have been painted in the fourteenth century. Using polarized light microscopy he identified tiny pigment particles of red ochre and vermillion (early paint pigments). He found no indication of blood on any of the samples from the image area. He was denounced by many scientists who believed the image was a genuine image of Christ emblazoned on cloth, formed perhaps 2,000 years ago. Many years after McCrone's work, the technique of carbon dating was applied to a few samples of the cloth. This technique relies on the principle that materials from living things, in this case plants, take up carbon while they are alive and stop when they die. As time passes, a small amount of carbon-14 isotope (an atom of carbon with a nucleus of different mass) decays slowly, but constantly. The amount of carbon-14 present is proportional to the age of the material. The technique has been refined over the years and is actually quite accurate and well accepted by scientists worldwide. The carbon dating results of the shroud from three independent laboratories closely agreed with Dr. McCrone. By using microscopy he had estimated the year 1355 as the date of the painting. The three labs arrived at 1325 by the carbon dating method.

MULTILAYERED PAINT
Above: Illuminated from a light source in the base of the microscope, a chip of paint with dozens of layers glows brightly. *Below:* The exact same view but this time illuminated from a light source above the paint chip. By simply reversing the illumination direction a huge difference is made in the appearance of the object under study.

The cream-colored powder

The first item we'll look at from our crime scene is the odd powder recovered from Richard and Ralph's shoes. The powder looks like the powder we've seen inside gelatin capsules or what might be left if a tablet were crushed. It doesn't look like the typical cocaine or heroin powder that we often see. There isn't much to work with so we'll have to be very careful and use microtechniques. This means that every test we do will use the absolute minimum amount necessary.

This powder is so minimal its analysis cannot be routine. We'll have to bypass our usual procedure of screening, identification and confirmation tests. They simply require too much sample. Our first test should be nondestructive, giving us as much information as possible. We'll use the IR microscope. If we don't get any satisfaction, we haven't lost any evidence and can retest using other methods.

The graph which the IR microscope produces is disappointing at best. It doesn't depict anything we recognize. After analyzing thousands of drug cases, we've learned to recognize the common drugs like cocaine and methamphetamine right away. This one looks really strange. We could look through a printed library of compounds, or we could let the computer do a search. Between the computer and printed library we are limited to only about 2,000 drugs, plastics and other compounds.

The computer search isn't much help, so we'll try another kind of test. In a later chapter we'll show how drugs form microcrystals when combined with certain solutions. Other kinds of chemicals form microcrystals too, their crystal shapes being highly characteristic of their chemical composition. We remove the particles we analyzed with the IR microscope and place them on a glass slide. We need to reserve some of the particles because the microcrystal test we're about to perform is destructive. Next, we dissolve the particles in a tiny droplet of dilute hydrochloric acid, about as strong as stomach acid. This is to get the particles into solution ready for the test. Then we place another droplet of platinic chloride next to the first droplet. Platinic chloride is a solution of platinum and is as expensive as it sounds. Using a sharp toothpick, we carefully draw the two droplets together and quickly place the slide under the microscope.

The point where the two droplets touch instantly turns a brilliant yellow color. Now we're getting somewhere. When viewed at 100 times normal size, the yellow color is seen to be made of thousands of microscopic octahedra (OK-ta-heedra). That means we see crystal shapes having a kind of octagonal pattern in three dimensions, resembling little faceted gems. They are also indicative of only two things: ammonium or potassium. Whatever this stuff is, part of its molecule has to be made of either ammonium or potassium or both.

This microcrystal test was published in 1953 by Dr. Paul Kirk, a pioneer in criminalistics. Even in the age of computers and expensive instruments we can still gather much information using the older but reliable tests. No machine can ever replace the logic and careful observa-

TINY GEMSTONES
Crystals of ammonium platinate form into characteristic octahedral shapes. The shapes of these crystals are the result of the efficient packing of molecules of ammonium phosphate in platinic chloride.

tions of a human examiner. But what does it mean? We have to find out why an ammonium compound would be found on both our suspect's and victim's clothing.

Viva la difference

Neither ammonium nor potassium would be present by themselves, as they make up only part of a whole molecule. As an example, table salt is really sodium chloride, an atom of sodium linked with an atom of chlorine. We can detect the presence of either sodium or chlorine and report our findings even though we know that pure chlorine or pure sodium is not present. The same principle applies here. If ammonium is present, or potassium, it's there along with the other half of the molecule. The crystal test we used was only able to detect the potassium or ammonium but couldn't distinguish them.

Ammonium compounds release ammonia when mixed with a strong base such as lye (sodium hydroxide). Potassium compounds don't release

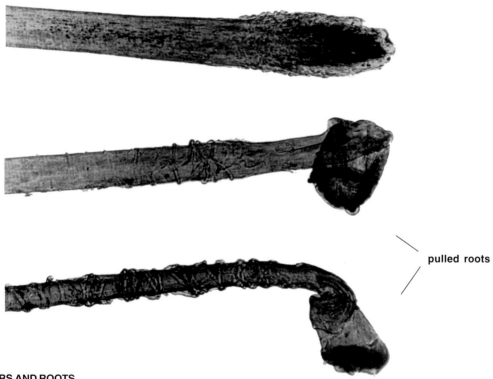

pulled roots

HAIRS AND ROOTS

By their microscopic appearance, human hair roots indicate how they were removed. When growing hairs are pulled out by force, their roots have flesh still attached *(lower two)*, but if they just fell out *(top)* after their growth cycle was finished, they have a distinctive rounded appearance. Hair comparison can include or exclude a person but can't conclusively identify someone unless some unusual feature is present.

potassium, and we'll take advantage of that difference by suspending a drop of platinic chloride solution on a glass slide upside down, hanging over a small amount of our unknown powder/lye solution mix. This technique is appropriately named the "hanging drop." If present, the ammonia vapors will combine with the platinic chloride and form the same microcrystals we saw when we mixed the two directly.

When we do the test, the hanging drop shows microscopic yellow octahedra just like before. We now know that our unknown has ammonium as part of its molecular structure. Armed with this new information, we go back to the published IR data, this time restricting our search to ammonium compounds. It isn't long before we find a perfect match: the published IR data for ammonium phosphate looks exactly like our IR data, peak for peak.

We suddenly realize that this powder is practically identical in color to the paper backing of the sticky tape we use to collect evidence at the scene. It would be virtually invisible if we didn't know to look for it. When we re-examine our tape lifts, this time turning the tape at an angle under the low power microscope, we see the powder all over the place. It's on all of the tape lifts from the body, sofa and carpet.

Research

To find out why this chemical might be found on someone's living room carpet we turn to a new item in the lab's arsenal, the "net." The internet, when used properly, can be of great value to us in searching for obscure information. Really an informal hookup of universities, manufacturers and government agencies, the internet has become a powerful tool in the lab. By now, millions of people have experienced the "World Wide Web," a more commercial and personal aspect of the internet. When we run into something unusual in the course of an analysis, we can enter a few appropriate keywords into a search program, go on-line and look for any occurrences of the keywords.

When we enter the terms "ammonium" and "phosphate" together we are given a list of possible uses, most commonly fertilizer and dry chemical fire extinguisher powder. Dry chemical extinguisher powder makes perfect sense. Somebody probably tried to put out the fire next to the sofa with a fire extinguisher. A call from us to the detectives sends them back out to the house to look for an extinguisher. We've used these extinguishers before and there should have been powder everywhere. Perhaps the pressure was low and the extinguisher old, allowing only a "puff" of powder to come out.

In a matter of hours a fire extinguisher is located under Richard and Lisa's kitchen sink. It's a good thing we hold murder scenes secure for a few days after our initial processing, never knowing what else we might have to search for. Sure enough, there are fingerprints all over its smooth, painted surface. The pressure gauge reads zero. Why people would save an empty fire extinguisher is beyond us. By swabbing out the nozzle and testing the residue using the same approach as we used on the powder from the tape lifts, we find no chemical differences between the two. We can't call it a "match" because ammonium phosphate is not distinguishable from one source to another. There are probably tens of thousands of these extinguishers around. It's just another piece of our complex puzzle.

Friends in the business

Knowledge is power and we can't overemphasize the value of having outside sources of information to aid us when we come up against a difficult question. In this case the internet came to the rescue, but what if we needed to know if any other criminalists have analyzed residue from a fire extinguisher before? The net is good, but it isn't that good. For specific information about what other forensic scientists have discovered we turn to the published scientific literature. Many articles on forensic science are within the pages of journals dating back fifty years or more. Every few months new journals are published by various organizations, such as the American Academy of Forensic Sciences and sent to crime labs around the world. If we develop a new procedure or discover a new substance we have an obligation to share it with our brethren criminalists. Beyond that, if we ever hope to introduce the new subject or technique in a courtroom we are duty bound to have others in the field review the procedure first.

Before an article is accepted for publication it must be peer-reviewed. This means the article describing the new topic is sent to prominent, well-respected members of our profession. They pick over the article, pointing out areas which are unclear or need more explanation. The editors of the journal wait until the techniques and articles have been polished before they agree to publish the article. When the article finally appears in print it is an achievement worthy of real professional pride.

GLASS CHIPS
The brittle and hard nature of glass causes conchoidal fractures to appear along the edges of these chips. The curve and shape of these fracture lines can give clues about which direction forces were applied when the glass broke. (Ruler lines are millimeters.)

BLUNT INSTRUMENT

When an object like this two foot long crowbar is wielded as a club and used to strike another person, blood may be transferred to the painted surface. Chips of the paint may also become transferred to hard objects which were hit. ·

The blunt instrument

Turning our attention to the items submitted as possible murder weapons, we see immediately that none of them is covered in blood. The detectives would have called that to our attention anyway. The crowbar does have some suspicious smears of reddish material, however. In addition, the color of the crowbar is closest to the paint chips from the skull, so we select it to examine first. Its surface is too rough for fingerprints to be recoverable, but it can still tell us a good story. We'll make an educated guess about how it might have been held if used as a weapon. The curved, hooked end is heavier than the straight end, so it was probably wielded as a club, being held by the straight end. The wounds on Richard's head would have been much more severe if he had been hit with the hook instead of the back of the curved end so we'll concentrate our exam on the curved area first. The whole length of it is covered in a light coating of frost, having just been removed from the freezer where it had been stored in the property room. After it thaws out we'll swab the smears and analyze the swab for blood.

A sample is taken of the blue paint from the area near the curved end. A sharp scalpel is used to flake off a little of the paint and place it on a microscope slide. We are able to hold the bar under the low-power stereo microscope to aid our sampling, and as we do so, we notice something interesting. Just about four inches back from the curved neck of the bar we see a dull silvery smudge. The paint is scratched all over the bar, but this smudge is about a half-inch long and could be a transfer of aluminum metal from the window frame. Unfortunately this bar won't fit into our scanning electron microscope, the instrument we would like to use to analyze the smudge. We could chop the bar into small sections with a hacksaw and analyze them one at a time, but the district attorney would lose a dramatic court exhibit, and we doubt he would approve.

To get a few traces off of the bar, sticky tape is pressed against the smudge and pulled away quickly, like stripping off a bandage. A few microscopic flecks of metal are transferred to the tape. In addition to the silvery metal, we notice dull white granules. These could be glass powder. At the microscopic level the force of breaking a window is considerable and glass, which has the same hardness as steel, can become imbedded in a metal object. The tape now has much of the trace evidence on it and we can easily examine it in the SEM and light microscope.

The scanning electron microscope lets us zero in on the metal flecks on the tape. Instead of light waves the SEM uses an electron beam for illumination, allowing it to magnify objects over 100,000 times if necessary. This technology has a few drawbacks and some important advantages. The physics of electron beams don't provide color so all of our images are rendered in shades of grey. The equipment needed to keep the instrument going is considerable in both size, complexity and cost. The advantages, though, include the ability to magnify images many more times than light microscopes and to see the surfaces in fine detail. In addition, when chemical elements are bombarded with electrons, an energy "signature" is given off that can be detected and analyzed by a computer for elemental identification. The combination of high magnification and elemental identification makes this device one of the most powerful in the lab. We zero in on a single tiny particle of metal and see aluminum registering prominently on the SEM's computer screen. There are micro-crystal tests available for aluminum but the SEM is nondestructive and allows us to get our elemental identification and still preserve the sample for later testing if needed.

Powdered glass

A few particles of the powdery substance from the bar are picked out with a needle and placed on a microscope slide. Under the polarized light microscope we see nothing but a dark field of view. This darkness means that the particles are not able to influence polarized light. Many transparent substances glow colorfully under these conditions. The fact that our sample is dark tells us that the powder is probably glass.

To rule out table salt and the few other substances that have no effect on polarized light, we take one of the two polarizing filters out of the light path. This is simply a matter of sliding a circular filter attached to the scope out from under the sample we're looking at. Without this filter in place, the scope acts like a regular light microscope. The particles have a curved, sharp appearance, showing what are called conchoidal (kon-COID-al) fractures. It is typical of glass particles to break randomly and with sharp, flaky edges.

Glass is a transparent substance that bends light according to its physical properties. The measurement of the light-bending ability of a substance is termed refractive index. Materials with a high refractive

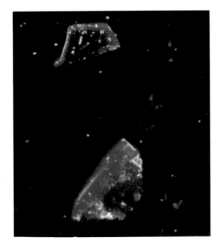

NOT REALLY A STAIN AT ALL, the technique of dispersion staining takes advantage of the prism-like effects of the edges of glass chips when surrounded in a fluid of similar refractive index. Here, a chip from crime scene evidence *(top)* is edged in a similar blue color as a chip from a victim's clothes. This finding suggests a similar origin for the two chips but can't be called an exact match.

index, such as a diamond, bend light dramatically. Air, having a low refractive index, has little effect. When lead is added to glass it increases the refractive index of the glass. That's why leaded glass sparkles more than regular glass and is used in chandeliers or crystal goblets. We can measure the refractive index of glass particles found on the crowbar and compare them to the samples of window glass we collected at the crime scene.

There are instruments that automatically determine the refractive index of glass chips, but since our lab doesn't have one of those devices yet, we'll establish the refractive index of the particles using the microscope. A chip of glass is placed into a drop of a specially made oil, called immersion oil, then examined under the microscope to see if the glass chip "disappeared." If the refractive index of the oil matches that of the glass, the particle will seem to actually disappear. We have a set of oils made in gradually increasing refractive index that can be used, then rinsed off and the next one applied. It's a trial and error process that takes a long time to complete. The light from the microscope is filtered during this process so that only one color is allowed to illuminate the sample. This avoids erroneous determinations as no two colors or wavelengths of light are bent at exactly the same degree.

After the refractive index of each sample is determined, we may compare the particles using a technique called dispersion staining. This procedure in misnamed, as there really isn't a stain as we might use for looking at cells. The color comes from the way the edges of the sample act like tiny prisms. It works best when the sample, in this case glass, and the liquid we added to it are almost the same refractive index. This liquid is similar to an immersion oil and can be rinsed off so it's not destructive at all. The liquid is a heavy, oily substance but a perfectly clear fluid about the consistency of vegetable oil.

When the glass chips are placed in a drop of the dispersion liquid on a microscope slide the edges seem to glow with shades of blue and yellow. A simple device is placed in between the lens of the microscope and the sample, blocking stray light from interfering with the delicate colors. The only light that makes it to our eyes are the rays which were bent, or dispersed, by the glass-fluid combination. It may sound complicated, but an effective demonstration of this technique has been displayed at many high school science fairs.

Using these microscopic techniques we find that the glass chips from the window and fragments picked out of the crowbar are similar in refractive index. Still we can't call it a match, since glass is a mass-produced item and there are undoubtedly thousands of windows with a similar type of glass. By this test we have, however, eliminated thousands of other possible sources of glass that would not have shown a similar refractive index. The range of alternative explanations for how all of the evidence got on this particular crowbar is getting pretty slim.

Shogun

Finding glass particles embedded in steel might seem unlikely at first, but we've seen some bizarre examples over the years. In one memorable case a man caught his wife with her lover and chased them around the house with a cheap samurai sword, swinging at everything in sight. When we examined the sword for blood we found no traces as he had, thankfully, only intended to terrorize his victims, not turn them into sushi. Embedded in the steel blade were numerous samples of powdered glass from more than one of the windows in the house.

Bathrobe

After tape lifts are taken of Lisa's bathrobe it is shaken carefully over a large piece of white paper. Sparkling glass chips are gathered up. She was in the room when the window was broken and we are not surprised when these chips agree in refractive index comparison to the window samples. When a window is smashed, numerous microscopic particles are sprayed in many directions, forward and back. Most of the large pieces may be forced forward, but the strain on the glass as it fractures propels chips in a backwards manner often lodging in a person's hair, shoes or clothing.

Paint chips

The paint looks very blue under the light microscope, especially when lighted from above using the coaxial illumination describer earlier. These paint chips aren't very transparent, so we don't try to light them from below like we would with cells or glass. Carefully, we've mounted a chip from the crowbar on a slide and adjacent to it a chip from Richard's skull. They are side by side, almost but not quite touching. Here's where we can get mixed up if we're not careful. A Polaroid photo of the ar-

SLICED WITH A RAZOR, a fiber's distinctive cross section is made visible. Although most are finer than a human hair the shape and chemical makeup helps in their identification. Synthetic fibers may come in a variety of forms, a few cross sections of which are sketched above. The rounded triangular shapes are called tri-lobal.

rangement is taken to help us recognize the shapes of the chips. We must not forget which is which. Next to each other they appear indistinguishable in color. This isn't conclusive, but it is important. The IR test we used to compare the paint is colorblind, so if we didn't look with our own eyeballs first, we could inadvertently "match" two different colors of paint. Such a finding wouldn't add to our credibility very much.

The IR works best on substances containing carbon atoms, referred to as organic compounds. Plastics, solvents, drugs and foods are examples of organic compounds. The IR isn't as good with inorganic or non-carbon containing compounds. Rocks, glass, and metal are examples of these. The pigment and other added materials called extenders can be studied using the SEM just as we did for the aluminum smudge. Many pigments and extenders are inorganic and contain trace elements such as titanium, calcium, zinc and magnesium.

The SEM identifies iron, silicon and magnesium in our sample. The iron could be from the bar itself, the magnesium and silicon could be from the paint. Both samples of paint show these three elements.

On a dented area of the bedroom window frame at the scene are small transfers of blue paint. After another half-day of testing we find no chemical or visual differences between this paint and that on the crowbar using the same analytical approach as with the other paint evidence.

We have established the crowbar as the instrument used to smash glass and leave paint chemically indistinguishable from items at the scene and on the victim. The crowbar is the probable murder weapon. Later, we will test it for blood traces. There is a two-way transfer of evidence: Paint from the crowbar is on Richard's skull and the window frame. Aluminum, arguably from the frame, is present on the crowbar. Monsieur Locard would be proud.

Bits and pieces

In addition to relatively straightforward crime scenes where hairs and fibers are collected and compared, the trace evidence section occasionally examines scenes where explosions have occurred. These kinds of scenes can be dangerous and may only be processed after the bomb squad or other authority declares the area safe to enter.

A bomb can be thought of as a device built with the intention of causing an explosion. This sounds obvious, but there are lots of things

which blow up. Compressed gas cylinders, even plastic pop bottles can explode with great force, and yet don't include the traditional ingredients commonly associated with bomb-making, such as gunpowder. An explosion can be thought of as a chemical reaction involving the rapid expansion of gases, usually associated with the release of heat.

In order for some bombs to function, they need a confined space and something to generate a lot of pressure very quickly. Pipe bombs fit this category quite well. They are usually made from short lengths of steel pipe, filled with gunpowder and capped at both ends. Sometimes nails are added to increase the bomb's deadly effect. A hole is drilled to allow a fuse or detonator to be fitted. When this kind of device explodes, gunpowder residue, fragments of pipe, chunks of circuit boards from timers and pieces of batteries are scattered in the wreckage. We collect as many parts of the bomb as we can find. Many explosives dissolve in water and we can gently rinse the pipe fragments with water and place the extracted residue on a microscope slide. Crystals characteristic of explosive components can be observed under the microscope if they are present even in minute quantities. The water soluble nature of the residue can spell trouble if the bomb caused a fire at the scene and the fire department sprayed lots of water on the bomb fragments making it more difficult to recover explosive residue.

When bodies are recovered from a bombing scene, they are X-rayed at the morgue. The dense tissue of a human body is often able to absorb shrapnel and other important pieces of evidence that might link the builder of the bomb to the incident. A tiny scrap of a timing device with a serial number or some other identifying mark could be recovered from a body.

Other types of explosives including TNT don't require confinement to work. They generate so much shock and pressure just by their chemical reactions that it doesn't matter if they are confined.

Major bombing incidents like acts of international terrorism are beyond the scope of a local crime laboratory's expertise. Those kinds of cases are usually referred to a larger agency with greater experience and resources. The larger agencies like the FBI (Federal Bureau of Investigation) and the BATF (Bureau of Alcohol, Tobacco and Firearms) labs have extensive libraries of clocks, batteries, wire, explosives and substances including military formulas that would be too difficult for a smaller lab to maintain. We don't mind deferring to our colleagues on these kinds of cases.

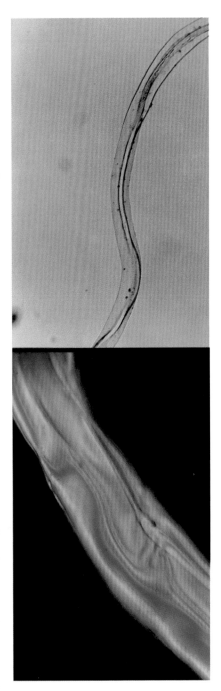

MICROSCOPIC CHARACTERISTICS are one way criminalists determine fiber type. Fibers found on tape lifts from a victim's clothes are identified by polarized light microscopy. *Top:* A garment fiber under normal transmitted light at low magnification. *Above:* The same fiber as it appears magnified and sandwiched between polarizing filters. This is an example of a tri-lobal fiber made of acrylic.

8

Blood Will Tell and Tell

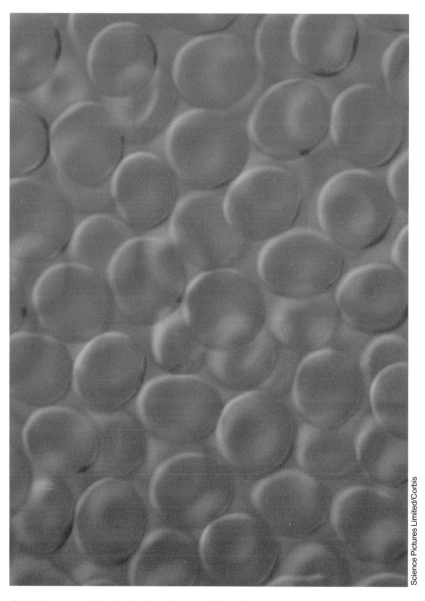

Fresh human red blood cells. Each hemoglobin molecule carries oxygen on an iron atom which produces the bright color.
These cells have lost their nucleus and thus have no DNA.

Wouldn't it have been great if Richard and Lisa's assailant had dropped his wallet at the crime scene as he made his hasty escape? A lucky break like this happens so rarely that it makes the news when it does. Now imagine the same criminal leaving behind thousands of tiny copies of his driver's license all over the place. Each one would be traceable back to its owner. That's what happens when DNA is used to identify people. Everyone flakes off skin, sheds hairs, ejects saliva when speaking and secretes semen or vaginal fluids All of these substances contain cells loaded with unique genetic material. Cell don't have license numbers stamped on them so we can't look up a DNA type and tell who left the evidence—not yet anyway. Banks of DNA data are being gathered for identification purposes and advocates for and against this process are lining up on either side of this politically charged issue. Everything we touch—our clothes, toothbrush, the fork we used at the restaurant last night, may have our own unique cells on it.

Currently, law enforcement personnel record the DNA types of persons who have been convicted of crimes, especially involving sexual assault. It allows them to use the information for future reference in an investigation. There is some pressure to not include the names of people who may have had their DNA typed because they were involved in a case, but not convicted of a crime. This might include the victim and anyone else who was requested to give a blood sample for instance, a lover or spouse, so comparisons can be made.

The blood stains

We can't assume that the blood smears and stains found throughout the house came from any particular person in our current murder investigation. We must be methodical and scientific in our approach. First, when we notice a red stain, we need to ask, "Is it blood?" All of us have been fooled at one time or another by animal blood, food, chemicals, makeup, even stage blood. But we take no chances. As we did at the crime scene, we'll perform a screening test, or "presumptive" test on a tiny portion of the unknown reddish substance. We have at least two types of screening tests. One is fairly specific but not very sensitive, the other incredibly sensitive but rather nonspecific. We could do both, but we have other tests we can perform.

In the near future blood testing at the crime lab will probably all be done by a DNA procedure. In a single DNA test we could confirm that the substance was human and identify whose it is. Right now, DNA testing is costly and it would be useful if we could screen out nonhuman blood and substances before wasting the time and expense of doing a full-blown DNA test. Occasionally, a sample simply lacks enough DNA to provide a conclusive result.

First, is it blood?

Unlike things which may look like blood, real blood contains cells rich in hemoglobin, the oxygen carrier and chemical that makes blood red. When blood dries, the cells shrivel up and aren't recognizable under the microscope. There were lots of stains at our crime scene which were probably blood, but before collecting any of them we performed screening tests. This was the test procedure in which a chemical turned blue indicating that there might be blood present. When blood is indicated, we take the stain to the lab and check for hemoglobin using the antihuman hemoglobin test. There have been many times an anxious detective has stood by waiting for the lab to confirm blood on a suspected weapon or article of clothing. The more quickly we provide information, the more value we have in the eyes of investigators.

Second, is it human?

To understand how the antihuman hemoglobin test works, we must briefly discuss the concept of antibody response. When we receive a vaccine against polio or tetanus, for example, we are actually getting a weakened form of the virus or bacteria. Our bodies react and attack the foreign proteins that surround the disease-causing agents and chemically "memorize" this experience. We are said to be "immunized" against the disease. If our bodies ever have contact with this live virus or bacteria again, we produce substances called antibodies that grab hold of the bacteria or viruses, rendering them harmless. The science of immunology was developed from the discovery of this antibody response.

Many decades ago scientists discovered that when an animal, such as a goat or rabbit, was injected with a foreign substance it would produce antibodies to fight the intrusion. The foreign substance, called an antigen, could be a drug, cocaine, or even blood from humans or other animals. The antibodies that the animal makes only react to a substance exactly like the one that was originally injected. The animals aren't hurt by this procedure; as a matter of fact, they are well taken care of, as they are very precious to the companies that keep them. Crime labs purchase antibodies specific for blood from chickens, cattle, cats, dogs, humans and indeed every animal that could bleed at a crime scene. We also purchase antibodies specific for human hemoglobin.

Once, we investigated a murder scene in a butcher shop. It was quite a chore sorting out the human blood from all the beef, pork, chicken, turkey, and lamb blood on the many sharp knives present. Another case involved a suspect arrested shortly after police found a severely beaten man. The fellow insisted he was innocent, but his clothes were stained with gory spatters of blood. We tested numerous blood sample from his garments using our antibody method until it became clear that the police should be looking for a cut up chicken instead, and this suspect was released.

How it's done

We only need a speck of blood small enough to fit inside this "o" to get good results. We'll run tests on all of the bloody evidence collected at our crime scene, including the towel from the kitchen, the broken glass from the bedroom, the telephone, a few spatters from the walls and ceiling, Ralph's shoes and, of course, swabbings from each of the possible murder weapons submitted for examination. The glass shards from the bedroom window did not test positive for blood, so they will not be tested further.

We've already prepared a microscope slide by covering it with a jellylike compound called agarose. It looks like cloudy Jell-O. Into this gel we have cut little holes down to the glass of the slide. They are the same diameter as this "o." We've cut two rows of holes about half an inch apart. The left row is for the samples, the right for the antisera (AN-tee-seera). Antisera are liquids containing the purified antibodies. We'll run known human blood on the same slide to act as a control sample. If the control doesn't come out positive, we'll know something's wrong with our procedure and reject the results of the whole test.

The loaded slide is hooked up to a 100-volt power supply. The electric current forces the antisera towards the unknown blood evidence and the unknowns are forced towards the antisera. If we had not used the electricity, the test would take much longer. Where the two substances meet, in the gel between the holes, is where the test is read.

Keep in mind that the antibody against human hemoglobin is extremely specific and will not combine with anything else found at a crime scene. If it finds its mate, human hemoglobin, it will form an insoluble complex, seen as a thin line of white material that can't be dissolved. We can stain this line blue to make it easier to see. When we see the line, it means that human hemoglobin was present in the sample hole. All of our samples show a positive result. It's no real surprise about these crime scene samples, there was obviously a lot of blood shed there, but we can't skip this step. How would it sound in court if we were asked, "You mean you haven't even proved it was human blood?"

The baseball bat, wrecking bar and hammer all show no results. The curved end of the crowbar is positive for human blood and so are the stains on Ralph's shoes. This is interesting; however, it doesn't prove he did it. The crowbar, remember, was recovered from Richard's own garage. Strong assumptions may be made from this result, and we are careful not to release any information until we've had a chance to narrow the number of possible sources of this blood. Right now, we've only narrowed the list of potential suspects down to the human race.

Distinguishing characteristics

Around the year 1900, a scientist named Karl Landsteiner discovered that mixing the serum (the clear fluid left after blood clots) of one person with blood from another sometimes caused the blood cells to clump together and sometimes did not. This observation he relegated to a brief footnote in a longer scientific paper he was writing, but this discovery of blood types was a turning point in the history of modern medicine. It paved the way for successful blood transfusions, human genetics studies and, most importantly for us, the ability to tell bloodstains apart. Here was a genetic trait which could not be observed easily, such as differences in hair and eye color, but required a lab test to prove. No suspect could disguise his blood type. Even though we still couldn't conclusively identify an individual, we could eliminate someone as having been the source of a bloodstain. If a person has a different blood type, he couldn't have supplied the blood in the stain. If he has the same blood type he *may* have supplied it.

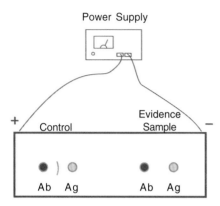

DETERMINING THE SPECIES of origin is accomplished by reacting the unknown antigen (Ag) with a known antibody (Ab). In this example the antigen is blood found at a crime scene and the antibody is antihuman antiserum. The small line forming between the two spots on the left indicates human proteins are present in the control. The lack of a similar line on the evidence sample is proof of a nonhuman source.

As DNA testing becomes faster and cheaper, bloodstain evidence will be analyzed by DNA methods alone and crime labs will gradually phase out testing for blood groups. Given sufficient evidence, it makes sense to screen evidence using "traditional" methods before performing the more specific, yet far more costly DNA testing. For example, if we can show that a suspect could not have left a bloodstain because he is a different ABO blood type, we can save a pile of money by not using DNA testing. It's only when we can't distinguish between a person's blood type and blood in a stain that we need to go further in our testing. If, at any stage along the way a person is eliminated as having contributed a body fluid, we cease further testing of that person. Biological testing is conclusive for eliminations. If the blood types match, then the person is only *included* in the suspect group. More about that later.

After Landsteiner, twenty-four years would pass before scientists would figure out how ABO types (blood groups) are passed from parent to child. The human population is, with a few exceptions, divided up into four groups: *A, B, O* and *AB*. There are numerous blood types and groups which can be tested for, including the Rh factor (the positive or negative often mentioned along with blood type), but these four are the principal types used in the crime lab. Everyone has two genes for blood type. Genes are bits of inherited information which tell the cell how to respond and create a characteristic. One gene is inherited from each of a person's parents. People with blood type *A* may have gotten an *A* gene from their mother, one from their father or both. If they got an *A* from mom they may have gotten an "*O*" from dad. The blood group "*O*" really means "no blood group." There are, therefore, three possible arrangements which lead to group *A* blood. Using two letters to show the person's genetic makeup, we say the person is either *AO, OA* or *AA*. Since we can't tell here which gene came from which parent, there is really only *AO* or *AA*. Both of these arrangements, called genotypes (GEE-no-types), will result in a person's body producing type *A* blood. It's the same story for type *B* blood. People with type *O* blood received neither an *A* nor a *B* from their parents, an *AB* person got one of each.

This is another turning point, as now we have the basic theory behind paternity testing. Keep in mind that there are enough exceptions to the rule that modern paternity testing now uses DNA typing. We can demonstrate a few clear examples using the ABO system.

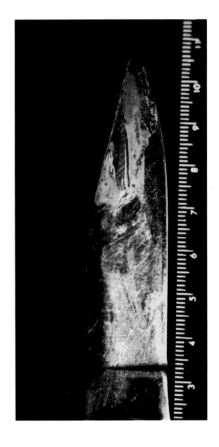

REDDISH SMEARS ON OBJECTS like this pocket knife must first be identified as blood, then as human and finally compared to a victim or suspect. Swabbing the smear for testing may destroy other information such as the depth of penetration or fingerprints. Accurate photographs must be taken prior to sampling.

Who's the dad?

Suppose a type *A* mother produces a child with type *B* blood. If she claims that a man with type *A* blood is the father, he can relax. The child would have *A*, or *O* type blood if that were true. Remember, each person has two genes. The mother must be an *AO*. If she were an *AA*, the child receives one of those genes, an *A*, from the mother no matter what, and could not have only type *B* blood. The child also should have inherited either an *A* or *O* from the accused father. The child can only be *AA* or *AO*, both of which make type *A* blood. Where did the *B* type blood come from? The real father must have contributed a type *B* gene. He could be *BB*, *BO* or even *AB*, since he only gives the child one of his two genes.

At a professional seminar, a young lawyer was having trouble grasping some of these truths. He asked, innocently, "Can't we verify the paternity testing procedure by taking a family where we *know* who the father is and test the blood from everyone and compare it?" The instructor shook his head and said, "We can never *know* who the father is with as much certainty as who the mother is." Still the lawyer persisted, "But, I mean, if we took a good family where we *really knew* who the father was . . . ." He still didn't get it.

It's the same with bloodstains. We weren't present to see who dripped the blood, but if the bloodstain is from a type *O* person, all *A*, *AB* and *B* persons can be eliminated as having left that evidence. This is conclusive, and eliminates about half the population. It's of limited value in identifying an individual because if a type *O* person is developed as a suspect, he and any other type *O* person could be the source of the blood. Of course that's not exactly true since there are millions of people who couldn't physically have been at the location where the blood was deposited, but that's more of a logical argument than a biological one.

The population is not evenly divided in ABO types. About half of us are type *O*, about one in three type *A*, one in ten or so have type *B* and the rest, about one in thirty, have *AB* blood. This is both good and bad. The good news is that the ABO system divides the population roughly in half. There's a fifty-fifty chance of a person being either *O* or something else. We like to be able to distinguish things, and we want to eliminate those not involved as early as possible in an investigation. This system does that nicely. The bad news is that there's a pretty good chance that more than one person in a case will have the same ABO type.

Getting mixed up

This whole process gets troublesome when dealing with mixed stains. We can't always tell if an *AB* stain came from a type *AB* person or a mixture of *A* and *B*. If the weapon had been used to beat a number of people it could be a real problem. The limitations of ABO typing are what helped motivate the development of more specific tests such as DNA typing.

Who's blood?

Blood comes to the crime lab in one of two ways, dried and liquid. Smears and drops of blood take only a few minutes to dry, so most of what we recover at a scene is dried blood. In order to establish an individual's own blood type, we have a nurse or technician draw a sample of liquid blood from his or her arm. These "standard" bloods are submitted to the lab in the victim and suspect kits we mentioned before.

It isn't hard to find out which ABO group a liquid blood sample belongs to. In fact, it's a regular exercise in many high school biology classes. Blood clots quickly once it comes out of the body, so chemicals are added to the tube to prevent this. Blood clotting is a complex series of reactions, each one depending on the one before. The chemicals added to the tube interrupt the series and the blood stays in liquid form. When we spin the blood tube around in a centrifuge it separates into two layers, a clear, straw colored upper layer, called plasma, and a dark red lower layer that has all of the red blood cells. We separate the layers and save them in plastic containers.

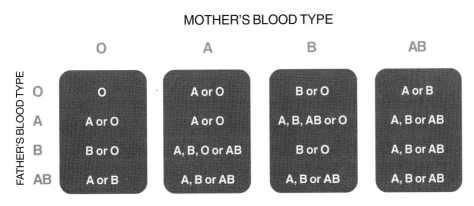

MOTHER'S BLOOD TYPE

FATHER'S BLOOD TYPE	O	A	B	AB
O	O	A or O	B or O	A or B
A	A or O	A or O	A, B, AB or O	A, B or AB
B	B or O	A, B, O or AB	B or O	A, B or AB
AB	A or B	A, B or AB	A, B or AB	A, B or AB

BEFORE DNA TESTING the ABO blood types of children were often used as evidence in paternity suits. The chart illustrates how parents of each ABO type could or could not produce children (in green boxes) of various types. The ability of two type *A* parents to produce a type *O* child is explained by the two parents possibly possessing an *O* gene as well as an *A*. In that case each parent would have contributed an *O* to the child.

To be extremely certain that we identify the correct blood group, we test the red cells and the plasma separately. Plasma (similar to serum but still containing all of the clotting factors) contains antibodies against blood types foreign to the person. People with type *A* blood have anti-*B* antibodies in their plasma and people with type *B* blood have anti-A in theirs. The plasma of a type *O* person has both anti-*A* and anti-*B* antibodies and the plasma of a person with type *AB* blood doesn't have any of these antibodies.

Remember the wound on Lisa's wrist? She was bleeding at the scene and we must determine the blood types of anyone who could have left a stain. Each "bleeder" must be included or eliminated by one means or another, and the ABO system is great for doing this cheaply and quickly. To determine her blood type, we'll need to dilute her red blood cells with a little saline, making a cherry red solution. A drop of this red solution is placed in three places on a glass plate. To each drop of cells we add a drop of commercially prepared reference plasma, one drop of anti-*A* and one of anti-*B*. The commercially obtained plasma is dyed blue for type *A* and yellow for type *B* to minimize mix-ups.

In a few minutes we see that the neither the mixture of anti-*A* and red cells nor the anti-*B* mixture has done anything. She could be a type *O* person, and to be certain we'll test her plasma as well. Testing the plasma is called reverse blood grouping. When we test the red cells, it's called forward, or direct, blood grouping.

To test her plasma we have commercially prepared reference cells. These are dilute solutions of red cells from people whose blood type is known. We'll do the test the same way as before only this time we'll use Lisa's plasma to get the antibodies and commercial reference cells to identify the blood groups. After only a few minutes we see a clumping of the plasma, reference *A* and reference *B* cell mixtures. That means there were anti-*A* and anti-*B* antibodies in her plasma. She is typed as blood group *O*.

Dried out

There are lots of variations on how to ABO type dried blood, but one way to do it begins with a thread. Dried blood can be moistened with water and absorbed onto a short piece of clean thread about a half inch long. The substances which give blood its ABO type now cling to the thread. Next, we tack three threads down on a plate of clear Plexiglas using nail polish. We must use three threads for each test, one for each blood type *A*, *B* or *O*. This procedure might require more blood than is found in some small spatters. If we can't spare enough blood for the ABO test, we'll skip it and go directly to DNA.

The plastic plate with the threads is ready for the next step. The same reference plasma containing the anti-*A* and anti-*B* that we used to type the liquid blood is pressed into service again. A single drop of anti-*A* is placed on the first thread, and one of anti-*B* is put on the second. People with high amounts of these antibodies in their blood sell their plasma to lab supply companies; in turn they will purify it for us to use.

Group *O*

How do we test for type *O*, the "nonexistent" blood type? There really isn't an anti-*O*, so we have to be clever about this one. A drop of a special compound called a lectin (LECK-tin) is placed on the last of the three threads. Lectins are chemicals produced by a plant and react chemically as an antiserum would. This lectin responds to a substance present in the *O* blood type. It turns out that the two blood types, *A* and *B*, are made in the body from the same preliminary chemical called "*H*" substance. Both *A* and *B* blood types start out as *H*. As they develop in the body, they become either *A* or *B* depending on the person's genes. In a person with type *O* blood, the substance never goes beyond *H*. If we find only *H* substance, but no *A* or *B*, we say that the bloodstain is from a type *O* person. Everyone has a little *H* in his or her body fluids, but type *O* people have only *H*. There isn't a very good source of true anti-*H* antiserum, so we use a lectin which is quite good at indicating *H* substance as if it were really an antiserum produced in an animal.

Each row of three threads on the plastic plate represent a single evidence item under test. Also present are controls and blanks. Blanks are clean threads with no blood, tested to show if there is anything on the cotton threads themselves which would interfere with this very sensitive test. Controls are threads swabbed on areas of the evidence item that are free of blood and act as a check for some substance on the evidence other than blood which might influence the test. In addition to all these samples, one thread each from a known group *A*, group *B* and group *O* person is run. It is important to see that the test is working correctly before any results can be interpreted.

Antibodies added to blood on thread

Antibodies attach to antigen in blood

Unattached antibodies are washed off

Reference cells added to washed thread

Attached antibodies are eluted off thread with heat

Released antibodies agglutinate (clump) matching reference cells

The whole test is known as the A/E or absorption/elution test. We are conducting the absorption part now. The antibodies in each antisera are looking for their counterparts in the blood soaked up on the threads. Anti-*A* is looking for type *A* blood, anti-*B* for type *B*, and so on. We don't know which blood type we might find, so we have to use all three. If anti-*A* finds type *A* blood, it will attach itself firmly to the bloody thread. If it does not, nothing will happen and it will be washed off. The same applies to the other two antisera.

The washing step involves nothing more than rinsing the plate off with chilled saline. All of the unattached antibodies go down the drain. Those antibodies that found their counterparts remain attached no matter how vigorously we wash the plate. You see, it's not the washing that can get the antibodies off of the bloody threads, it's the temperature.

Elution means to remove into solution. By letting the plate dry and then carefully placing a single drop of saline on each thread, we give the antibodies a place to go when they come off. The plate now has blood soaked threads, three for each stain to be typed. One of the three threads has both blood and the corresponding antibody. We can't tell by looking, but the blood type of the blood has already been determined. The only thing left to do is find out which of the three threads, *A*, *B* or *O* has antibodies attached to it. We place the plate into an incubator for a few minutes and gently warm the threads, antibodies and saline. Like magic, the antibodies are released from the blood and float into the saline.

Next, we remove the plate from the incubator and place blood cells from known blood types into each drop of saline. Just as with the antibodies, one drop of type *A* reference cells is placed into the saline of the thread which had type *A* antisera added before. To the thread that had been treated with type *B* antisera, we now add a drop of type *B* reference cells, and known type *O* reference cells to the thread treated with the lectin. Now we wait.

After a few minutes in the saline drop next to the thread taken from the crowbar, the type *A* reference cells are forming a little clump. It looks like a tiny blood clot. The same thing is happening in the *B* drop, but not much is happening in the *O* drop. What is occurring is this: The antibodies which were taken up by the blood have been released back into the saline. They were then free to react with their counterpart reference cells. Any anti-*A* antibodies that encounter a couple of type *A* cells will form a bridge between the two of them. More and more cells become linked until there is a clump big enough to see without a microscope. Those threads that didn't take up any antibodies, either because there was no blood on them or because the blood was of a different type, show no clumping On our blank threads there was nothing to react with the reference cells, so nothing happened.

Blood, sweat and tears

In the saliva and other body fluids in about four out of five people there is a substance corresponding to the person's ABO blood group. These people are termed "secretors" since they secrete their blood type into their body fluids. Saliva, tears, sweat and semen all may contain their blood type substances. This could be a problem if the sweat of a secretor interferes with blood found on an item of evidence, usually clothing. This is one reason why we run control samples taken from blood-free areas on the items we test. If the controls come out negative, then we can be assured that the blood type results are from blood and not a combination of one person's blood and another's sweat.

Results are in

Our control threads come out negative. If we had tested Ralph's undershirt or socks we might have seen some sweat contamination. The crowbar has type *AB* blood on it, a fairly rare type—sometimes we get lucky, as only about five percent of the population possess this type. We concede that this stain could be a mixture of *A* and *B*, but on Ralph's shoes we have type *AB* blood too. Unlike the crowbar which had a smearing of blood, the shoes have clearly defined spatter stains, and we typed the blood from only one of those spatters. Technically, the A/E test can't tell if the blood was from an *AB* person or a mixture of *A* and *B* type bloods, but the way we sampled the evidence gives us confidence. The only way the stain we just typed on the shoes could be from more than one person is if the blood was mixed prior to it being spattered. The circle of evidence implicating Ralph begins to close. Ralph and Lisa are both type *O*, the most common ABO type. This is probably enough evidence to hold him over for trial, and we'll make a call to the district attorney at this time. Also, spending the money to perform a DNA test is justified. Many labs have eliminated the ABO testing altogether, but it will be a few years before all of them do.

	GROUP		
	A	**B**	**0**
Positive controls			
known AB	4	4	1
known O	-	-	4
Blanks & negative controls			
Blank thread	-	-	-
Crowbar control	-	-	-
Ralph's shoe control	-	-	-
Blood evidence			
Crowbar	4	4	1
Ralph's shoe	4	4	1
Reference samples			
Ralph P. standard	-	-	4
Lisa W. standard	-	-	4
Richard S. standard	4	4	2

THE RESULTS OF TYPING DRIED BLOOD by the absorption/elution method are tallied in the chart above. The samples are grouped according to their role in the test. Positive and negative controls establish that the test is functioning correctly. The numbers refer to the relative amount of clumping seen in the indicator cells added during the last step of the process, '-' is negative, '4' is complete clumping.

9

Life's Little
Instruction Book

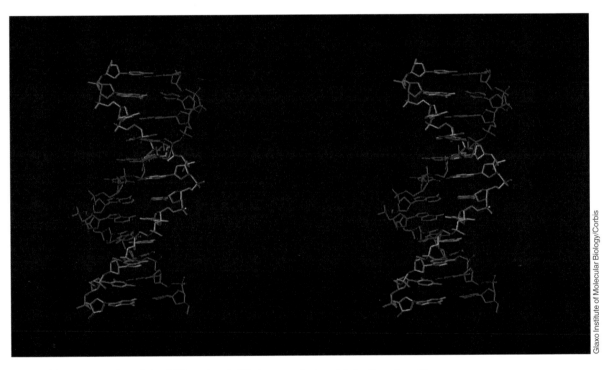

A colorful representation of the DNA molecule, this model shows only two tiny fragments of the whole length. The red and blue halves can be separated with enzymes, each half being a perfect match for the other. The image can be seen in three dimensions by gazing between the left and right models until a third appears to "float" above the page.

ADVANCED BIOLOGY

Each of the billions of cells in our bodies work together like a miniature factory, pumping out proteins, hormones and other products essential for our life. This they do under the instruction and guidance of a molecule called deoxyribonucleic acid (dee-OX-ee-rybo-nu-KLAY-ic) or DNA. This molecule is remarkably long and contained within the nucleus of every cell. Two exceptions exist: Red blood cells and cells forming the outer layers of skin lose their nucleus (and therefore their DNA) during their life-span. Bone, skin, liver, kidney, muscle and nerve cells for example, contain the same DNA that every other cell has. It's truly marvelous how a heart cell can have the exact same DNA as a brain cell yet "know" how to pump blood and not do arithmetic.

Everyone begins life from a single egg and sperm cell. Half of the DNA in any given nucleus came from the mother's egg and half from the father's sperm. After conception it is simply a matter of cells dividing. Biology is the only science where multiplying and dividing are the same thing. No more DNA was added to or subtracted from each cell. Each "daughter" cell, as they are called, gets an exact replica of the DNA present in the cells before it. Everyone's DNA is a little bit different from everyone else's, everyone except for a clone. An identical twin is a kind of clone, and since an identical twin separated from the original egg and sperm combination, we can see why they would have the same DNA. Fraternal twins don't have the same DNA, since they came from two different eggs and sperm.

We all have two eyes, two arms, a mouth and so on. We differ in the details. The DNA that codes for the mouth and fingers, arms and legs is pretty much the same from one person to another. A small amount of DNA doesn't seem to code for anything yet differs from person to person. Remember, half of this DNA came from the mother, half from the father. Think of a deck of playing cards. The whole deck represents the total DNA for that individual, and each card represents a distinct DNA code. The deck gets shuffled as it passes from one generation to the next.

The joker is wild

Everyone has his or her own deck. After thoroughly shuffling the cards we notice that there are more than two jokers scattered throughout the deck at various places. The number of cards between jokers varies from deck to deck. Imagine a test that only looks for jokers. The test cuts the deck whenever it finds a joker; the result is a table covered with little stacks of cards, some with a few, some with dozens of cards to a stack. Each stack begins with a joker and the sizes of the stacks are the "profile" of the person's deck.

The DNA test works like that. DNA is isolated from a blood or semen stain and treated with enzymes. The enzymes act like chemical scissors and "cut" the DNA molecule every time they find a group of DNA codes which act as a flag. The "flag" DNA codes would be like the "jokers" in the deck. The amount of DNA in each resulting snippet varies from person to person just like the piles of cards on the table. Measuring and counting the lengths of snipped DNA fragments, we obtain the person's DNA profile.

Dozing off

Late one night, in our city, a woman, Lynda A., stabbed a man to death in a little hamburger stand. As he struggled with her, he managed to grab strands of her long, brown hair. When they found him the next day he had a couple dozen hairs still clutched in his stiff fingers. The roots from these hairs contained cells that were typed for DNA. A match was made between the hair roots and the suspect, leading to the first DNA-based criminal case of its kind in our state. In accordance with the defendant's wishes no jury listened to this case, only a judge. Highly complex tests such as this require great effort on the part of expert witnesses to explain technical details to a judge or jury. A recent issue of the famous satire magazine *MAD* included a cartoon where a DNA expert in a murder trial was patiently explaining to a jury how the techniques were performed. The jury in the cartoon was bombarded with so much technical information they were bored to tears, fidgeting and trying to stay awake. Unfortunately, it sounds all too true.

Extract, snip, sort

Scientific analysis often involves separating complex mixtures. We have already described how the gas chromatograph separates chemicals and drugs but blood, hair and semen won't go through such a device easily. In order to separate these materials we first extract the DNA contained within their nuclei using chemicals. Then using enzymes, the DNA is cut at predetermined points. Those points are the "jokers" we referred to in the deck of cards example. Finally, we sort the fragments according to their size using a technique called "electrophoresis" (electro-for-EE-sis). This exotic term really just means to "move through by way of electric current."

To understand how electrophoresis works picture a group of people trying to run through a densely wooded forest as fast as they can. Each person carries a stick held horizontally across his chest. Some have sticks as long as they are tall, while others carry sticks only a foot long. Everyone starts at the same place and time. Will they all be able to pass through the forest at the same speed? Of course the runners with the shortest sticks will pass through more easily. This is the principle of gel separation techniques such as electrophoresis.

In the lab our "forest" is a thin, flat square of gel, maybe a foot across. First we load our samples, placing them into evenly-spaced areas at one end of the flat gel "plate." Electric wires are placed at each end of the plate and the power is turned on—usually several hundred volts for many hours. After a while the short molecules have gotten past the gel molecules and gathered farthest from the starting point. They collect together from their repulsion and attraction for the electricity and according to the chemical properties of the gel. The molecules of greatest length have barely even moved. There are several variations on this theme, but this is the general idea.

After the electricity is turned off, and we look at the plate, there's not much to see. The molecules we are testing for aren't visible without some help, so we place a thin membrane on top of the plate. The membrane, called a blot, is coated with special DNA that exactly corresponds to the short sections of DNA that should be on the plate. This is called a probe. The term probe refers to a chemical probe and is simply a way for us to see how far the molecules travelled along the plate during the time the electricity was on.

The probe DNA is commercially manufactured DNA that is the "complement" to the DNA fragments on the plate. The term complement means that the probe DNA will match up to the codes of the fragments exactly, similar to the way a glove might be a complement to the hand that fits it. We already know which codes to expect, that's not the unknown part. What is unknown is how many and how large the fragments are for our particular sample, and where they ended up on the plate. Attached to the probe DNA is an indicator chemical. This could be either a mildly radioactive substance or a colorizing chemical. If a piece of X-ray film is pressed flat against the probe, any radioactivity will cause tiny areas of the film to fog. When the film is developed we can see the famous "bar code" look of the DNA test. Each dark band shows where lots of DNA fragments are and how far they travelled.

The evidence sample only takes up a small area on a plate and there's room for more than one test. We always save room for controls, samples with known origins. They are from donors or commercial suppliers and are run in several places on the same plate. We also need to establish what our victim's and suspect's DNA types are, so we run them at this time as well.

The DNA film is called an autorad, meaning "self-radiation." Looking at the film from above, reading from the top down, there is a marker, Richard's standard blood sample, Ralph's standard blood sample, another marker, the blood spot from Ralph's shoe, a third marker, the swabbing from the crowbar and a fourth marker. We run known DNA fragments as markers, nicknamed "ladders," at various places on the plate in case one side of the gel wasn't exactly the same as the other. The dark bands might shift up or down a bit and the ladders show where DNA fragments of varying lengths line up. We can get a rough idea of how long our unknown fragments are by comparing them to the ladders.

If the test is a disaster, say, the gel dries out or cracks, we'll just reject it and do it over. If there isn't enough evidence left to do it again, we may have a problem. Usually, we can tell before we run a test whether there will be enough material collected from the crime scene to run more than one test. We owe the defense one-half of the evidence, and must get permission from the prosecutor before commencing a test with the last remaining bit of evidence. This applies to all testing in the lab, not just blood. Sometimes the defense will have their own criminalist observe us if only one test can be run.

Planning ahead

Why run Ralph's blood standard? After all, he wasn't the one who was bleeding, in fact, he showed no wounds of any kind when he was arrested. The answer is that if he were to offer a reasonable explanation for the blood on his shoes as being from his own nosebleed, for example, we could immediately refute or support it. If we hadn't tested his blood we'd have to admit that his story was possible, even if remote. The type of DNA test shown here, the RFLP test, takes a couple of weeks at a minimum, and many labs are backed up for months. There simply isn't enough time during a trial to do the testing again.

Bins, bands and big debates

The position of the dark-colored bands, how far they've travelled along the plate, gives them a value. Within predefined limits, a band may be assigned a number or letter identifying it as a certain DNA type. Once the whole plate is "read" we can compare the DNA types to other cases or even a national database like the FBI's CODIS system. (CODIS is the Combined DNA Index System established under the DNA Identification Act of 1994.) Just how wide those predefined limits are drawn is the subject of much debate. Both law enforcement and defense experts are struggling to find a fair way to assign values to those little bands. The more loose the definition of what constitutes a certain value for a band,

THE RESULTS of an RFLP DNA test are seen in this piece of film called an autorad. Slightly radioactive chemicals attached to DNA fragments link up to the evidence DNA and expose the film in dark banding patterns. Every few samples is separated by a marker, a standard mix of DNA fragments of varying sizes. The markers help spot problems with the gel used to do the test.

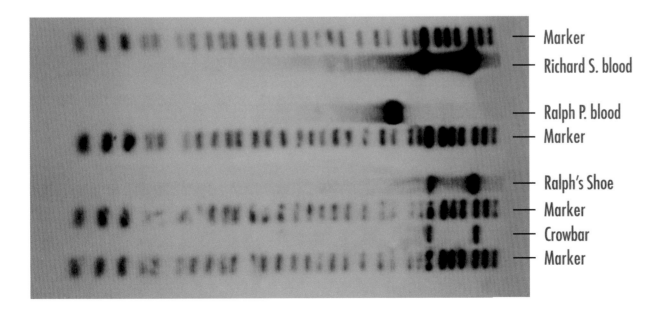

— Marker
— Richard S. blood
— Ralph P. blood
— Marker
— Ralph's Shoe
— Marker
— Crowbar
— Marker

the less discrimination ability the test has. To explain by way of example, suppose we have two buckets, and into each one we toss a pebble. The rules state that only pebbles weighing an ounce or less go into bucket number 1, called grade 1 pebbles. Into the other bucket go all other pebbles. Those are grade 2 pebbles. There are an awful lot of pebbles that could make it into the grade 2 classification. OK, let's increase the number of buckets to twenty. Grade 1 is now any pebble weighing less than an ounce, grade 2 includes only those from 1-2 ounces, grade 3 from 2-3 ounces and so on. Now we can distinguish between twenty different classes or grades of pebbles.

It seems that it would always be better to have more classes. But where do we stop? Getting back to DNA types, how many buckets or "bins," as they are called, is a good compromise between practicality and fairness? The defense argues that there should be fewer, wider bins, so lots of people are lumped together as having the same type. The ability of the test to separate two different people would be fairly poor. Prosecutors want more and smaller bins, so that practically everyone is distinguishable. This simply can't be done as there are only so many bands that can fit on a plate of gel. What if a band shifted up or down just a little bit, maybe due to a slight imperfection in a gel? A band could be placed into an inappropriate bin and be incorrectly identified. If there are few bins, there won't be much point in storing the results in a database, as practically everyone will match everyone else. Only experience will sort out a compromise that is right and just.

A little goes a long way

The DNA test we've described was originally developed in the 1980s and known as the RFLP (Restriction Fragment Length Polymorphism) test. Restriction fragment refers to the snippet of DNA cut by the enzymes. Length polymorphism refers to the fact that these snippets vary in length from person to person. It requires a relatively large amount of sample, say a dime-sized blood or semen stain or lots of hair roots. Often a crime scene sample is less than that so we need a way to test small samples.

One of the unique things about the DNA molecule is that it will make copies of itself. Remember how every cell in the body has an exact copy of the DNA made from the sperm and egg uniting? It's the ability of the DNA molecule to reproduce itself that makes this possible. The DNA molecule looks like a long, twisted ladder. The rungs of the ladder can be made to split apart right down the middle, creating two complimentary halves of the ladder. Think of two halves of a torn page, the zigzag tears matching exactly.

In 1984, research scientists found they could take advantage of DNA's copying ability in a process called PCR (Polymerase Chain Reaction). DNA extracted from only a few hair roots or a few sperm cells was placed in a device called a thermocycler. This is just a carefully controlled heater that raises and lowers the temperature over and over. Enzymes were used to make the DNA molecules copy themselves, in a process known as amplification. When the process was complete, they found they had made useful amounts of DNA.

To understand what's happening, take the number one and double it. This represents the first cycle. Now double it again and again for twenty or so cycles. What do we get? 2x2x2x2x2x2.... We've quickly made a million copies of the original DNA. Only a short section of the whole molecule is used for this amplification. We start out with an insufficient amount to test and end up with more than enough. The resulting DNA product may be tested using a simple color-coded test called a dot blot, or the sample may be sent through a gel similar to the RFLP test for extremely precise results.

Diminishing returns

There is much care taken to ensure that only relevant, human DNA is amplified. It should always be a concern whenever an amplification technique is used that what is being amplified truly came from the crime scene. Another area of concern is when only a very few sperm are amplified. Remember how sperm cells and egg cells have half the amount of normal DNA? It's because they combine at conception to produce a single cell with the full amount of DNA. But this means that each sperm individually carries either the man's father's contribution or his mother's contribution to the particular DNA fragment we're amplifying. Stated another way, we want to amplify the man's full DNA type, not half of it. To do that

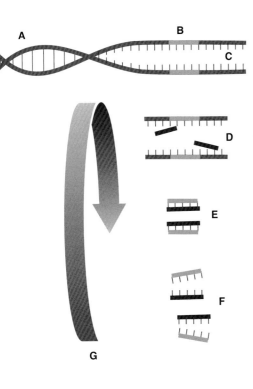

DNA'S UNIQUE ABILITY to make copies of itself is the principle behind PCR testing. Just doubling the target section of DNA twenty times can produce a millionfold increase in the amount available for testing. At the top is a sketch of a complete strand of DNA in its familiar double helix configuration (A). A target region of DNA is identified for amplification (B). Heating splits the DNA down the middle (C). Through a combination of enzymes and temperature cycling, DNA segments called primers attach and copy the target areas (D, E). Two new copies of the target DNA have been made (F) and the whole process is ready to repeat (G).

we need to use cells that have a normal amount of DNA already or enough sperm cells that it averages out. Since they are randomly mixed, a few hundred sperm cells should roughly represent the same DNA that we'd find in any of the man's other body cells. Analyzing only one or two could present a problem. This may seem like a fine point, but it's often forgotten in the drive toward analyzing smaller and smaller traces of biological evidence. Current PCR methods used in crime labs won't allow only one or two sperm cells to be amplified, although technically it is possible.

Out of this world

Once the unknown DNA types on the evidence samples have been identified we compare them to a larger group of people's types. This allows us to predict the odds of finding another person with exactly those same types. We can't test everyone on the planet, so we've developed a set of statistics that predict how often a particular type might occur. Ferocious court battles have erupted over how many other people need to be typed before it can be said how rare a certain DNA type is. Another source of great conflict in court is the astronomical numbers called frequencies of occurrence often reported when speaking of DNA tests. We offer a brief refresher in statistics to help the reader follow this controversy.

When a coin is flipped, everyone knows the odds of it landing on heads or tails is 50:50. Stated a little differently, the probability of it landing on tails is one chance out of two, or 1/2. If we flip two coins the probability that they will both land on tails is one in four, since they can only land in one out of four possible ways. This is the same as multiplying 1/2 by 1/2. The reason this works is because we say the coins are independent of each other. Neither coin cares what the other did; neither coin influences the other. This is the basis of the so-called product rule criminalists rely upon in blood typing cases. Extensive research has shown that many genetic traits are inherited independently.

A DNA type can be thought of as a trait, just as hair color is a trait. As with the coins, the probabilities of having each trait may be multiplied times the other traits to get a total probability for all of the traits appearing in one person. This won't work if two or more genetic traits influence one another, they must be independent. There are experts who claim that we simply haven't tested enough people yet to be sure we have independence. This argument and other, far more technical arguments will perpetuate court battles for years.

Big numbers

DNA reports are often full of seemingly impossible statistics such as, "one out of 60,000,000,000 people could have this combination of types." How can this be possible? A number like that is more than the population of the earth! It would probably be more understandable, if less accurate, to state this combination of types is so rare that there is probably no other living person with the same types. The way we generate those big numbers is the same way we multiplied the two coins, by multiplying together the frequencies of independent traits.

To explain further, let's develop a bank of information on people we have tested. This way we can make estimates of how rare a DNA type is when we encounter one in a criminal case. After a while we might have tested 200 people for a trait we'll call GREEN. It's a made-up name, but the idea is still the same as the real thing, just simplified a bit. Remember, the traits tested for in a DNA test don't show up as something you can see on the person's body like hair or eye color; they can only be detected by DNA tests. GREEN can be expressed in two mutually exclusive ways, either GREEN 1 or GREEN 2 and since everyone has two parents, they have two GREEN genes. We express the two together with a comma separating them. There are three possible types for the trait: GREEN 1,1; GREEN 1,2; and GREEN 2,2. Since we can't tell without testing the parents which type came from which parent there is no difference between 1,2 and 2,1.

People born with a DNA type of GREEN 1,1 are common folk. We're not commenting on their social status, but they make up sixty percent of the population. If we were to select any person at random, we'd expect to find a GREEN 1,1 type person more than half the time. GREEN 1,2 people are a little less common, about three of every eight. People with a GREEN type of 2,2 are a rare breed with only three percent of the population carrying this trait. With such a low percentage we'd be sur-

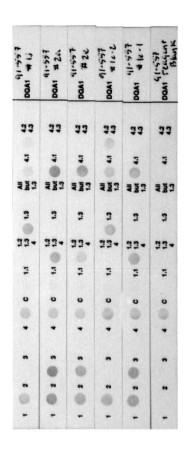

DOT BLOT
The results of a PCR test may be read as a series of colored dots on a strip of plastic. Above are six separate PCR results from five samples and a blank. The intensity of the color is related to the amount of DNA amplified during the procedure. The numbers refer to the DNA types, the "C" is a control dot which must be readable for the test to be valid.

prised to find more than one person in every thirty-four with the same GREEN 2,2 type.

We use the term frequency to mean how common a trait is. GREEN 1,1 has a frequency of 0.60 while the frequencies of GREEN 1,2 and GREEN 2,2 are 0.37 and 0.03 respectively. The sum of all of the frequencies adds up to 1.0. We'll need these figures later.

Because such a large part of the population is lumped together in the common GREEN traits, we'll need to use a second test, otherwise we might not be able to distinguish between suspects, victims and crime scene evidence. In a typical case, we wouldn't run only one DNA test. There are lots of similar DNA traits we could test for using a battery of different probes. The theory of each of them is identical, only the frequencies change. But we've already run a perfectly good test independent of GREEN—the ABO test which we did earlier. Let's use the two test results together and generate some numbers. From previous research we can be confident that ABO types and our GREEN trait are inherited independently.

When we tested our suspect, Ralph, we found him to be a GREEN 1,1. That's not surprising, it's the most common type. Lisa and Richard are both GREEN 1,2. That's good information and shows that we can separate all of the players using the two tests. Before we get confused, let's summarize:

	GREEN	ABO
Lisa	1,2	O
Richard	1,2	AB
Ralph	1,1	O
Crowbar	1,2	AB
Shoes	1,2	AB

Between the two tests, we can distinguish each person from the other. This is essential in sorting out what happened at the scene and who left the blood evidence behind. If these two tests weren't able to separate everyone we'd keep testing more and more traits until we could.

To calculate the combined frequencies of the two tests, simply multiply the individual frequencies together:

	GREEN	ABO	PRODUCT
Lisa	.37	.50	.19
Richard	.37	.03	.01
Ralph	.60	.50	.30

Under the heading "Product" we show the result of the multiplication. The smaller the number, the more rare the combination of types. Richard, as you can see, has pretty rare blood. In a random crowd of 100 people we'd only find one person with his combination of GREEN and ABO types. To get the number 100, we divided 1 (one) by the number in the column. One divided by .01 equals 100. Lisa and Ralph both have fairly common DNA types for GREEN and ABO. Rounding the numbers, it looks like one out of five people share the same types as Lisa and one out of three the same as Ralph.

If we tested a whole battery of traits using DNA procedures we may generate big numbers rather quickly. The numbers are just the results of multiplication problems, though, and may exceed the actual population of the world for really rare types. This is nothing to get confused about, it just means that some combinations of types in one person are unique.

Caveat

We must point out an important assumption when choosing which numbers to multiply. We said the trait was seen in one out of 100 people. Which people? Strong arguments are made during trials over which population the defendant's DNA type should be compared to. A type that is rare in the black population might be fairly common in Caucasians and never seen in some tribes in Australia. The defense may claim population data listing a DNA type as common, the prosecution may claim the more rare types should apply. It's not so easy to look at someone and assign them to a race. Some people may have reasons for claiming to belong to one group or another. Many people really aren't all that certain of their ancestry anyway. Another assumption is that people of different races freely mix and marry. While this is becoming more common, it is still true that people tend to marry within their own racial group. For years our crime lab compromised by averaging the local population and reporting that a particular type occurs in "X percent" of the people in "our county." We used a census report to find out the racial breakdown of our county and figured out how many people of each race would be expected to show a given type. Of course this approach has problems too. What if the person tested isn't from "our county?"

Name calling

The U.S. census is taken every ten years but many people move from county to county more frequently than that. The questionnaire used by the census bureau to report race information is filled out by individuals, some of whom wish to claim membership in a particular group. It isn't checked for accuracy, and there's really no practical way to verify the information.

There is an assumption by some scientists that there is a race called "Hispanic." We believe that this is not the case. Hispanic is an ethnic designation, referring to a people sharing a common language, heritage and culture. There are representatives from every race under the Hispanic umbrella. Famous people make our case for us. There are baseball players from the Dominican Republic who have Spanish surnames and speak only Spanish are certainly Hispanic, yet they are also descended from black African immigrants. Television shows originating from Mexico City star Caucasians of obvious western European heritage, yet how could they not be Hispanic too? Which database should we use to decide how rare or common their DNA types are?

Once, we contacted a prominent, private DNA laboratory with a question: "How is it decided when a person's blood test result goes into the Hispanic database?" We knew that this laboratory was building databases of hundreds of people to establish the frequency of certain DNA types. We were told, sheepishly, that a technician in an East Los Angeles blood bank looks at the last name of the donor and decides. "Yeah, there are probably a lot of Hernandez's and Sanchez's in there." We think the Hispanic DNA database should be abolished.

The motivation for all the controversy is simple: If the DNA test is accurate and correctly done, and the theory behind it sound, a few tiny cells can conclusively identify an individual out of everyone else on the earth, with that annoying little exception of identical twins, of course. This is bad news for guilty defendants and heaven-sent for innocent ones. With a test this powerful, both prosecution and defense must tread carefully.

Newest kid on the block

DNA testing revolutionized the field of forensic science practically overnight. Dozens of traditional blood typing tests, some quite involved and complex, became obsolete. The DNA test itself wasn't invented overnight of course. We borrowed many of the procedures from the field of molecular biology where they had been under development for some time. That's the way it's been for most of the history of forensic science. Our evidence is so varied that practically every scientific discipline is represented in our testing. Criminalistics doesn't receive the big research dollars that medical, nuclear, petroleum and aerospace research gets, but we aren't slow to recognize a good idea or piece of equipment when we see it. That's why it is important to have criminalists who come from a wide variety of industry and research backgrounds.

There is a tendency to believe that the latest technology will be the salvation for every problem and answer to every question. There is an undercurrent of resentment among some non-DNA-specialist criminalists who fear the sexy new technology will bleed off precious financial resources from traditional analyses of evidence like glass, soil and paint. DNA testing has it's limits and must be used appropriately. Like all tests it can generate lots of meaningless information. We need all of the disciplines in the crime lab to be supported.

We turn our attention to the white flakes and green plant material recovered from the tape lifts.

10

Chemical Vice

Heroin powder is often stored in toy balloons, each containing one dose of the drug. The heroin is shown here in brown powder form is only about 2% pure. Another popular form, "black tar" heroin, is much more potent.

Drug analysis

When it comes to drug analysis, criminalists become chemical detectives, usually performing a simple government regulatory function, but occasionally trying to outsmart an unpredictable illicit manufacturer. Prosecutors use the lab to establish the presence of a controlled substance to gain a conviction for drug possession. In 1970, congress made a schedule, or list, of five classes of compounds it deemed unlawful to possess, sell or manufacture. The lab's job is to decide if the substance the police seized is on the list. Much information can be squeezed out of a seemingly simple cocaine or heroin case by criminalists who care to do so.

A drug can be defined as a substance, other than food, taken to produce some effect on the body. All drugs, including antibiotics, heart medications and painkillers have a desired effect and one or more side effects. The federal government classifies drugs according to their potential for abuse. Drugs are considered to be abused when they are ingested (taken internally) for reasons unrelated to their intended medical purpose.

The classification scheme is federal but individual states may add other substances, as desired. The classification does not include over-the-counter drugs such as common cold medications, although if some of the active ingredients in those drugs were found in bulk quantities they might fall under a restriction. The ranking of the list has nothing to do with how dangerous a chemical is—cyanide, for example, doesn't even appear.

The lowest classification might be termed "by prescription only." This means in order to lawfully possess a specified substance a licensed medical professional acting within the scope of his or her practice must have prescribed it. Dentists can't prescribe birth control pills, but could prescribe codeine tablets for pain from a tooth extraction. The next five classifications are termed "schedules" and range from roman numeral V (five), the lowest, to I (one) the highest. Drugs in schedules IV and V have a low potential for abuse and include cough syrup containing a little codeine, and benzodiazepines (BEN-zo-dy-AY-za-peens) such as Valium. Schedules III and II include drugs which have a high potential for abuse but also have a legitimate medical use, such as cocaine, morphine and methamphetamine.

The schedule I group lists famous drugs like marijuana, heroin, LSD and psilocybin (sill-oh-SY-bin) mushrooms. Members of this elite group have been deemed to have no legitimate medical value, although a few exceptions have been granted. Some states are experimenting with the idea of allowing the medically approved use of marijuana. Also, members of the Native American Church are permitted to use peyote, a little ceremonial cactus that produces the hallucinogen mescaline.

The list is ever changing. As political pressure is exerted, more chemicals may be added to the list. Even chemicals which only theoretically could be made are found on some lists. A few drugs become elevated to higher classes and others demoted as fashions change and more research is done.

The schedules have little to do with the effects produced by the drug when ingested. The effects on the body are yet another way we lump drugs together. Stimulants speed up the heart and respiration. These drugs are the ones which are associated with a nervous person. Caffeine is one stimulant which doesn't even appear on any schedules—good news for coffee drinkers. Cocaine, methamphetamine and common cold remedies are also in this category.

Depressants and hypnotics are drugs that can make a person drowsy and even unconscious. Morphine, barbiturates, Quaaludes are some well-known examples. Antihistamines, simple pain relievers like aspirin, local anesthetics like benzocaine, antiinflammatory drugs, high blood pressure medication and antibiotics are not on the schedules and therefore of limited interest to the lab. Only in the case of a fatal overdose would the crime lab get involved in their analysis.

In the field

Even though we treat each item of evidence as a complete unknown, many items have been tested in the field by an officer trained to perform "presumptive" tests. Some courts allow defendants to be held over for trial on drug charges based upon these simple chemical screening tests performed in the field. Before a conviction can be obtained, the crime lab must finish the analysis, but allowing officers to screen unknown substances takes considerable deadline pressure off the crime lab as many defendants plead guilty at this stage. Small plastic bags containing the same chemicals we use in the lab for screening drugs are commercially manufactured and given to police officers to use. All the officer need do is put a pinch of the substance suspected of being a drug into the bag and crush the glass ampoule that is included. Powerful acids and chemicals go to work on the suspected drug. If a certain color appears, it's off to jail. In our state it's a crime to sell imitation drugs, so even a negative test won't always get a person off the hook. It depends on what promises and statements the suspect made if and when it was sold to an undercover officer.

The crime lab provides regular drug training to any officer who requests it. Mostly the training involves using authentic substances so the officer can testify in court that he or she knows what the real drug would do in the test kit, and compares this experience with what the officer saw in the field. Only rarely do we encounter a substance that tested positive in the field but came up negative in the lab.

Handlers of narcotic-sniffing dogs are supplied with authentic standards so the dogs can know what the real thing smells like. Only the crime lab is in a position to establish what the real standard is. We have the sensitive equipment which can verify the identity and purity of the compound. We also have a DEA (Drug Enforcement Agency) license allowing the laboratory to purchase pure drug standards from pharmaceutical companies no matter how high the federal schedule.

Inquiring minds

As part of a community service program, the lab provides a free analysis of suspected drugs brought in by worried parents. If parents find a capsule or green leafy plant under their child's bed, we'll either confirm their suspicions or grant them relief. These cases are given high priority. Even though they aren't strictly law enforcement related, we understand how important it could be to a family to have the answer before the child comes home from school. What a difference our timely analysis might make at the dinner table conversation!

How much is really there?

Many drugs are extracted from plants. These chemicals can exert powerful influences on the human body. Pure drugs directly extracted from plants often don't dissolve very well and are useless to the body if they're injected or swallowed. Coupling them chemically with a salt allows them to dissolve readily. An example of a salt would be hydrochloride. Cocaine hydrochloride is made of cocaine base and hydrochloride salt. Together they form cocaine hydrochloride, a chemical that is extremely soluble in water. Someone discovered that inhaling the vapor from heated cocaine base could produce more powerful effects than the hydrochloride and so began the fashion of free-basing. This means to remove the salt and go back to the base form of the drug as it was extracted from the coca plant. A simple chemical extraction was invented to dissolve the cocaine hydrochloride in water then extract it out in ether, an extremely flammable solvent. After some rather spectacular fires, this method was discarded in favor of a safer method using baking soda, the resulting product is nicknamed "crack" cocaine.

The total weight of the drug is influenced by the weight of the hydrochloride salt. Chlorine is a heavy atom and about twelve percent of the weight of cocaine hydrochloride comes from the chlorine in hydrochloride. Suppose a person was in possession of two ounces of cocaine hydrochloride which was fifty percent pure. Our state imposes an increased penalty for possession of over an ounce of cocaine when calculated as pure. No problem, since fifty percent of two ounces is still one pure ounce, right? But chlorine isn't actually part of the cocaine molecule, so it really shouldn't be used to increase the weight. The actual total weight of the cocaine alone is 0.88 ounces, well under the one ounce limit.

Are we beginning to sound like defense experts? Sometimes the prosecutors think so. We like to think we're arguing what the evidence really shows, not for or against either side. If the defendant had three ounces of this stuff, we'd be right there proving that he had more than the requisite ounce of pure cocaine base. It's really a question of mathematics and chemistry, nothing more.

The same logic applies when a police agency submits a sack full of marijuana for the lab to weigh and analyze. Marijuana is pretty easily identified, most of it consists of flowering tops of the plant. But what if the sack also contains stalks and roots as well as some of the drug-laden resinous leaves? If time permits we'll "manicure" the contents, separating out the inert parts and not include them in the total weight.

How much is enough?

Of the many issues confronting the drug analyst, usable quantity is undoubtedly the thorniest. The issue of usability is really more legal than scientific. Many criminalists won't even offer opinions in court about this topic. Over the years, the courts have struggled with the idea that to sustain a conviction for possession of a controlled substance, the quantity of the substance must be "sufficient for use." This brings a lot of questions into mind. What about a single seed from a marijuana plant? You can't smoke it, but it could grow into something that could be smoked. What about a perfectly good marijuana leaf encased in a solid, clear resin block for display at school antidrug education programs? Sure, it's a usable amount, but is the fact that it's totally inaccessible relevant?

Whether a given amount of drug is usable becomes subjective in some, but not all instances. In forming our opinion we study material the federal government publishes, chat with drug users and narcotic officers and maybe even observe people caught in the act of abusing drugs. We need to know how much people take, how they take it, how they save the remains after they take it and how they store their next dose. In the lab, we look at the evidence in question and attempt to manipulate it in the manner of known abuse, short of actual ingestion of course. Could a drug user successfully take such a tiny amount and make a cigarette out of it? Sniff it? Dissolve it in water and inject it?

Money laundering

Each criminalist will gradually form an opinion about what constitutes a usable quantity of a given drug. The personal ethics of the individual analyst will dictate the level of technology employed in recovering trace amounts. We have equipment in the lab that can easily extract microgram (millionths of a gram) quantities of cocaine from an otherwise "empty" paper bindle. We ask ourselves, "Is it reasonable to expect a drug user to manipulate quantities this small?" Using advanced chemical extraction techniques, we have even recovered trace amounts of cocaine from paper currency obtained from a bank. You couldn't see the drug and certainly couldn't use it, but it was there just the same. Is that enough for a drug possession charge?

Different drugs will have different cutoffs. Because of the different ways in which marijuana, for example, is consumed it would have to be present in quantities much greater than cocaine or heroin to be usable. Current methods of abuse are frequently discussed among forensic scientists and narcotic officers.

Packaging methods

Another consideration is the way drugs are packaged, legally termed "method of packaging." Here again the criminalist is asked to form a subjective, expert opinion. The method of packaging must be apparent as an attempt to conserve the substance, as opposed to leftover material. The operative question is, "What is reasonable?" A very large plastic bag which at one time held a kilogram (about two pounds) of cocaine might now have a thin film of residual dust clinging to it. A determined individual could perhaps recover a small bindle (folded paper container) of cocaine from that same bag by carefully scraping the sides of the bag. But this imaginary bindle was not submitted for analysis, rather the bag was, and it is up to the criminalist to decide if the residue is to be considered usable. We'll tell the prosecutor that if the amount of residue had been collected and placed in a bindle, it would be usable.

The dosage form must also be considered. A tablet or capsule is by definition a usable quantity. A loaded syringe may present additional problems however. A residual amount of liquid remaining in a five cc syringe which cannot be forced out through the needle might be usable if it were contained in a one-half cc syringe.

Consistency is an essential element of expert testimony. This is nowhere more evident than in cases involving usability issues. Every time we testify about usability, we keep a record of the amount of the drug involved. After a while, a "gray area" emerges between what we think are clearly usable and unusable amounts. That is our personal cutoff for a particular drug packaged in a certain way.

Red herrings

The issue of physiological effect is not relevant to the question of usability despite many attorney's attempts to make it so. Case law in our state is generally in agreement that the prosecution does not have to prove that the contraband possessed had a potential of producing a narcotic effect. Different people have different tolerances for certain drugs and it would be quite difficult to certify that a person received a physiological effect from a given amount of drug.

Another "red herring" frequently encountered in court is the percent purity argument. Suppose, one is often asked, that only a tiny speck of the drug was mixed with a hundred pound sack of sugar. Would this be usable? It is rarely necessary to know what portion of the powder in question is a controlled substance. It is sufficient in most cases simply to show that there was enough powder to manipulate in the manner of known abuse, that the screening and identification tests for the drug were positive, and that the drug was packaged in an apparent attempt to conserve it. It would be useful to know approximately how sensitive each screening test is, as the trier of fact (judge or jury) may feel reassured in knowing that these tests are not likely to detect tiny amounts of drugs mixed in with a hundred pounds of sugar. Some of the laws dealing with possession of controlled substances specify not more than an ounce or so of a "*substance containing*" the named drug, and thereby avoid the whole issue.

We use a three-step approach to the identification of a completely unknown drug. First the substance is screened to either include or exclude from the list of controlled drugs. Second, the identification step gives the chemical a name. At this point the drug is no longer an unknown. Finally, a confirmation test acts as a quality control for the identification step. The purity of the drug may be established at this time.

The screen

It seems like a daunting task, to take an unknown powder, tablet or liquid and tell it apart from the tens of thousands of chemical substances in the world. The way we do this is by cleverly taking advantage of the unknown's chemical properties. The flakes found on Richard's clothes are a solid white substance at room temperature. Right off we've eliminated thousands of chemicals which can only exist in liquid form at room temperature. We have also eliminated all chemicals which are colored other than white. The screening process functions as a massive elimination step. When we're done with the screen no drugs will have been identified but lots of unrelated chemicals will have been eliminated.

A few of the flakes are placed into several depressions in a specially made white porcelain plate. This plate is about the size of a butter dish and has eight or so depressed areas, called wells, to hold samples. A drop of screening test solution is dropped on top of the substance in the well. One of the solutions is actually concentrated sulfuric acid and it's not uncommon to find little holes eaten through our lab coat after a few days. Another screening test solution is made from the chemical cobalt thiocyanate.

The only screening test which gives a positive result on this white substance is the cobalt test. A brilliant, flaky blue reaction occurs in the porcelain plate. This is highly characteristic of cocaine. Even though we don't consider the screening test specific for cocaine, we've never seen a compound other than cocaine which gives the same degree of blue, the speed of reaction and that same flaky look. To merely report that the reaction is positive because the solution turned blue is to ignore all of the observations we actually made during this test.

The identification

We see crystals everywhere. A diamond is a crystal of carbon, an ice crystal is made of millions of water molecules all fitting together efficiently. Crystals are the most efficient way in which to pack molecules. Criminalists found that many drugs make crystals too, each one having a unique shape. When cocaine hydrochloride is mixed with a chemical called platinic chloride, microscopic crystals looking like molars are produced. When gold chloride is used as the chemical instead, sharply-pointed little crosses result. Heroin, when mixed with mercuric chloride, makes little sea urchin-shaped crystals. These tests, when done properly, are specific and rapid. Pure drugs form specific crystal shapes that cannot fool experienced examiners.

The key is working with pure drug samples. Drug evidence received by the lab is usually of poor quality. Cocaine, for example, is nearly always cut with various sugars or baking soda or other cheaper drugs. If we get an uncut package in its original brick form, the purity is dependent on the skill of the "factory" where it was produced. About a fifth of the total weight will be by-products and not cocaine. The microcrystal test may not work if the sample is too badly contaminated, weird fuzzy-shaped crystals may grow. We'll do a chemical cleanup that selectively separates cocaine and leaves the rest behind. A small amount of the powder is dissolved in a sequence of solutions and then dried back down to a powder. After the cleanup procedure, the crystal test is run again, if cocaine's there, we'll see it.

To perform the crystal test we put a drop of the dissolved cocaine on a slide and allow it to dry. A drop of crystal test solution, in this case platinic chloride, is placed next to the suspected cocaine. The drop of solution is drawn into the cocaine with a toothpick and the slide is immediately inserted under the microscope—these crystals grow quickly. What we observe are tiny crystals shaped like flat molars, one end flat and the other end with "roots." The shapes identify the substance as cocaine.

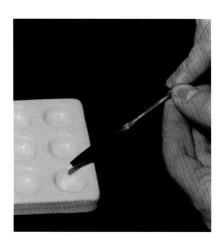

JUST A PINCH of the unknown is placed into a porcelain dish for the screening test. The amount of unknown drug seized for testing is usually so large that destructive testing is not a problem. When only traces are available, this method cannot be used.

Some crime lab managers feel like there's nothing for them to review when crystals are the only tests run on a drug sample. The test is destructive, so the little bit of drug that was used is gone forever and can't be retested. They may require that a confirmatory test be run on an instrument that produces paper they can look at and feel comfortable about. There will always be the need to trust the integrity of the analyst; we can't always photograph and print out everything we see. Much depends on the experienced eye of the one actually examining the evidence. Regular proficiency testing is the best way to verify the analyst's abilities.

The confirmation

The good thing about a confirmatory test is that it can serve double duty. We can design a test that not only verifies the identification made by crystals, but also gives a percent purity of the evidence. This information can be quite useful to narcotic officers working undercover. They can legitimately complain or brag about the quality to their drug "connection" without worrying about sounding like an idiot or liar, or worse, a

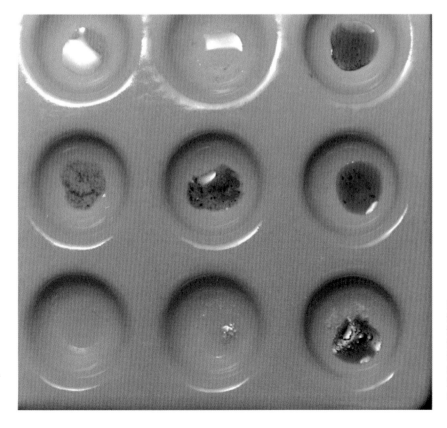

BRIGHTLY COLORED SOLUTIONS result from the screening test chemicals when they mix with drugs. Cocaine is indicated in the right upper and middle wells, heroin in the very center. In addition to the color, the nature of the reaction is important. An oily blue look in the right lower well is highly characteristic of methamphetamine.

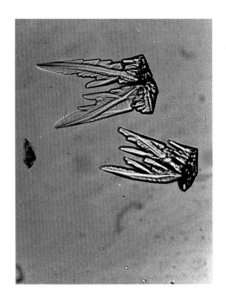

MICROSCOPIC SIGNATURE
Many drugs make highly characteristic microcrystals. *Above:* Cocaine hydrochloride microcrystals in platinic chloride solution look a bit like molars. *Below:* Heroin in mercuric chloride looks a little like sea urchins.

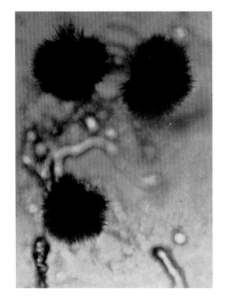

cop. It gives them that little edge of credibility. Also, information on drug quality can be used for intelligence gathering. There are networks of law enforcement agencies that keep track of the quality, quantity and price of drugs across large areas of the U.S. If the quality is steadily declining for example, and the price remains high, it may show that suppression efforts are effective.

Another side benefit to running a confirmatory test is the identification of excipients (ek-SIPP-ee-ents). These are inert bulking agents added to drugs to increase their weight. If an ounce of cocaine is cut with an ounce of mannitol (a kind of sugar) then profits double. Of course if the drug is cut too much, the customers will feel no effects. Lidocaine is a local anaesthetic similar to cocaine, but lacks the powerful effect and doesn't have strict government regulation. For this reason it is occasionally mixed with cocaine. Lidocaine will produce a numbing effect on the gums just like cocaine, so customers who casually test the mixture won't be able to tell how much it has been cut.

In the near future, GC/MS will conduct the automated sampling of hundreds of items of drug evidence. The only time-consuming step will be the careful preparation of the samples. The GC/MS will provide information on identification of the drug and its purity, without the need for a confirmatory step. Some cutting materials, like sugar, however, have difficulty going through the GC/MS without being chemically modified and will still have to be identified by other means, usually under the polarizing light microscope or IR.

The confirmatory test we have selected is the GC or gas chromatography test. To do this step we need to place an accurately weighed amount of the cocaine into a glass vial and add some alcohol to dissolve it. We don't use water because the material inside our GC column would not tolerate it. To improve accuracy, we use a very precise microgram balance. The amount we weigh doesn't matter as much as knowing exactly how much. This may sound strange, but no matter how much we use (within practical limits) it can be dealt with mathematically, but it's *knowing* the exact amount that matters. In this case we don't have much, so we weigh 0.1532 grams. That's about as much as a saccharine tablet weighs. We could have weighed more or less, but we need to know the exact number in order to calculate an accurate percentage later. Actually, that's about all we have of this substance. The flakes of cocaine are placed into the vial and the alcohol is added. The GC test is destructive, but only for the small amount we inject into the instrument. The rest of the cocaine and alcohol mix can be saved for future testing.

The alcohol that we added to the unknown isn't alcohol alone, it contains another substance, the internal standard, a precisely measured amount of another chemical that will be used to compare to the cocaine.

The GC shows that only cocaine and the internal standard are present. The concentration of the internal standard is already known but the concentration of cocaine is not. The mathematical ratio between the two gives us the percent purity of the cocaine. This sample works out to be about eighty-five percent pure. That's pretty high, we rarely see "street dope" more pure.

Green vegetable material

Most criminalists are not trained in the discipline of botany but there are a few examinations we routinely do that rely on the research of professional botanists. We found tiny fragments of green vegetable material on our tape lift of Richard's clothes. Under the low-power microscope we notice several distinctive features characteristic of marijuana. Ten or more years ago it became popular with defense attorneys to argue that there were more than one species of cannabis, and since only *Cannabis sativa* was deemed illegal, there was reasonable doubt as to which species the defendant possessed. Like most novel arguments, it faded away into obscurity, probably more due to the common usage of the stuff than because of massive research efforts. It is commonly held that there is one species of cannabis, but it can assume more than one form. Currently, the most frequently encountered form is called *sinsemilla* (Spanish for "without seeds"). It is distinguished from other forms by the huge amount of resinous, sticky material it forms on its flowering tops. The active ingredient, THC (tetrahydrocannabinol) is dissolved in this resin. Hashish, a concentrated form of this material is rich with THC and microscopic plant material as well.

Microscopically, the fragments are quite interesting, having stiff, hook-like hairs on the top surface. These hairs are called cystoliths (SIS-toe-liths) and resemble a rhinoceros horn in their proportions. In days past we would receive whole marijuana leaves for identification and we could quickly note all of the familiar characteristics, serrated leaves, long

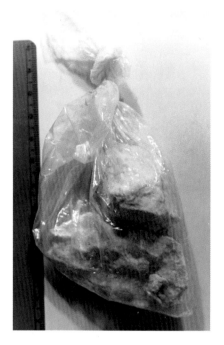

MIND ALTERING SUBSTANCES
Above: Chunks of uncut cocaine hydrochloride await mixing with inert compounds to extend their weight and dilute their concentration. *Below:* Peyote cactus, used in some Native American religious rites.

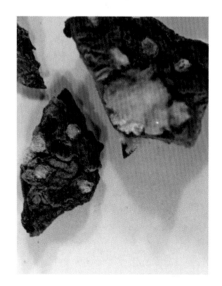

silky hairs in addition to cystoliths, and so on. Nowadays it is quite rare to find a whole leaf. Thus we need to rely on a combination of chemical and botanical tests to reach an accurate identification. The THC and similar compounds produced by the plant react to a curious solution of acid and vanillin. This test, called Duquenois-Levine, is probably the most pleasant smelling test we do in the lab. The vanillin reacts with THC in the plant fragments turning a deep purple. The final part of the test involves dripping chloroform into the tube. The chloroform, which is heavier than the blue solution, takes the color with it as it sinks and the test is read as positive. The two layers don't combine for the same reason that oil and water don't combine. The chloroform is heavier and insoluble in the vanillin-acid solution. If we needed to confirm the result, such as in the case where no plant material was present at all, we use the GC to look for the ingredient THC.

Poisons and drugs

Looking for drugs and poisons in the human body is one of the oldest specialities in criminalistics. Pathologists, medical doctors who study disease, have been interested in ways to identify foreign substances in blood, urine and other body fluids for over a century. In 1914, the Harrison Narcotic Act was passed. This resulted in lists of chemicals that the government declared to be illegal to possess. It was then necessary to develop a testing procedure to see if an unknown substance seized by police was on the list. Since that time, it's been a game of chemical cat and mouse with the clandestine drug chemists always one jump ahead. The law defines compound X as illegal, the illicit chemist alters the molecule slightly, and poof—we have a new, as yet unrecognized chemical, not on the list. Perfectly legal. Unknowing human guinea pigs eat the stuff or inject it into their veins and, if they're lucky, only experience the expected altered state of consciousness. Occasionally, something will go very wrong.

Designer drugs

A few years ago, a clandestine chemist was attempting to synthesize meperidine, a synthetic opiate marketed legitimately as Demerol. This fellow altered a few steps in what was a rather complex recipe, manufacturing a completely unintended side product. When people took his drug, they became frozen stiff, unable to move a muscle. The medical community was baffled. It was eventually discovered that by giving the patients a drug used in the treatment of Parkinsonism, L-dopa, they got better and became "unfrozen" for a time. Meanwhile an expert toxicologist at a crime lab in California was hard at work deciphering the structure of this as yet unnamed chemical. Remember how the GC/MS broke up molecules in a predictable way? This holds true even for unknown molecules. It may be that this dangerous side product will assist medical research into future Parkinsonism treatments.

Only recently has crime lab technology been able to keep up with the ingenuity of the poisoner or drug abuser. LSD, a popular hallucinogen, is usually taken in such small quantities, for example, that detecting it in the bloodstream was virtually impossible until a few years ago. Without demonstrating the presence of a named drug in a person's blood, it is quite difficult to prove the person was under the drug's influence.

Proving possession of a controlled drug follows the same logic. One of the things that must be shown by the state before a person can be convicted of possessing a controlled drug is that the drug was actually there. White powders look similar and even if they are claimed to be sugar, flour or cocaine, their identity must be proved chemically. It occasionally happens that a non-controlled substance is sold as if it were an illegal drug, bought and taken internally without the seller or buyer being the wiser.

We have identified two different controlled drugs present at our crime scene. Does that mean this could be a drug-related homicide?

Blood alcohol and toxicology

The body fluid samples from Richard and Lisa are going to be tested for alcohol and drugs. It could be argued that since Ralph was arrested hours after the incident that any substances we identified in his system might have been taken after the crime was committed. The body is continuously metabolizing drugs and alcohol, trying to eliminate them. One of the chief functions of the liver is to render drugs and alcohol harmless or at least in a form that can be excreted by the kidneys into the urine.

MARIJUANA (*Cannabis sativa*) leaves showing their distinctive serrated edges. The dark green surfaces of marijuana leaves have microscopic hairs, shaped like rhinoceros horns, called cystoliths.

Blood, breath or urine

The most commonly consumed drug by far is alcohol. Because of serious incidents caused by intoxicated person's operating machines such as cars, ships and airplanes, crime labs have developed a sophisticated method to determine a person's blood alcohol level quickly and accurately, even if no blood is sampled at all.

To find out how much alcohol a person has in his or her system, we'll need a sample of a body fluid with water in it. A large percentage of the human body is water, and it is water that mixes with alcohol. Blood alcohol level is the "gold standard," all other body fluid alcohol measurements being compared or converted as if blood had actually been sampled. When urine or breath is measured, the results are converted to an equivalent blood alcohol level by multiplying them by a predetermined conversion factor.

A glass of wine, beer or shot of whiskey each contain approximately the same amount of pure ethanol (the chemical name for the alcohol in drinks). In a man weighing 175 pounds an ounce of ethanol will raise his blood alcohol level to about 0.025 percent. The percentage is calculated

CHUNKS OF CRACK
Cocaine in base form, is "smoked" in pipes similar to the one shown. Unlike tobacco or marijuana, cocaine isn't actually burned in these pipes, the drug turns into vapors which are inhaled.

as weight-percent, that is, grams of alcohol divided by 100 milliliters of blood. For reference, think of 100 milliliters as about the volume of an egg and 0.025 grams as about as heavy as half a drop of water. Over the years criminalists and police simply refer to it as percent blood alcohol. The ounce of alcohol must have been consumed in about an hour to raise the man's level that much. If the man has a stomach full of food or if the alcohol is diluted and consumed over the course of several hours the level will never reach that high.

The body generally eliminates alcohol at the rate of about 0.02 percent per hour. This number is an average, and the rate is not influenced by strong coffee or fresh air. There's virtually nothing one can do to speed up the elimination of alcohol, only wait. The elimination rate has some interesting implications. If a person is arrested with a blood alcohol level of .24 percent at 1:00 a.m., and put into the "drunk tank" at the county jail and then released the next morning at 8:00 a.m., he'll drive home with a blood alcohol level of 0.10, still over the legal limit in many states. It takes a rather experienced drinker to get up that high in the first place, and when he leaves the jail he may not show the typical signs one

BUNDLE OF BINDLES
Torn from the pages of men's magazines, powdered cocaine hydrochloride is packaged in small folded paper bindles. The red "S/W" seen on the evidence tag indicates these items were seized by search warrant.

POPULAR HALLUCINOGENS since the 1960s, LSD *(above)* and the psilocybin mushroom *(below)*. The LSD is shown in "blotter acid" form. Each of the half-inch paper squares contains a single dose. Blotter papers are often colorfully decorated.

might associate with an intoxicated person. He will, however, still have the same inability to operate a car safely as if he had just reached the 0.10 level a minute, instead of hours, before.

The analysis of ethanol is pretty simple. There aren't any other solvents similar to ethanol which can be safely swallowed in amounts as large as ethanol. The breath alcohol measurement is done by sampling the deep, alveolar air. This is air from down deep in the lungs, brought up by exhaling fully for many seconds. The alveoli (al-vee-OH-lye) are the tiny sacs in the lungs which allow oxygen and carbon dioxide to pass into the blood. While those gases are transferring, alcohol is also passed out of the blood and into the moist air to be exhaled. This air sample is passed through a device that records the presence of alcohol.

Another way to determine the blood alcohol level is by taking a urine sample. This procedure is a little more difficult because we don't know how much urine was already in the person's bladder before he or she began drinking. The prior presence of urine in the bladder would dilute the alcohol and result in a falsely low reading. We ask the person to empty their bladder and then wait twenty minutes or so. The sample taken after that is the one we use for the analysis. This assures us that the urine used for the analysis is representative of the current blood alcohol level.

Blood, drawn from a vein by a nurse or doctor, and urine are both analyzed the same way; we use the gas chromatograph. In this instance there is a special material in the hollow column that can tolerate water, not like the substance in the columns used for arson or drug analysis. The GC oven temperature is kept fairly low as alcohol and water boil at fairly low temperatures compared to most other substances. The graph produced by the machine shows a peak proportional in size to the amount of alcohol present in the sample. We use an automated sampler which can test hundreds of samples in a day.

For medical examiner's cases like Richard, we may not have enough blood or urine (and we certainly can't get any breath) to do an analysis. We mentioned that any body fluid with water would also contain alcohol and there are a few more we can try including bile, brain, vitreous fluid (eyeball) and other organ tissues.

Lisa's blood alcohol result is 0.11 percent and Richard's, taken from blood remaining in his heart, is 0.07 percent. They had been drinking, but they weren't falling down drunk at the time of the murder.

Tox talks

That's not the end of the testing for these samples. Toxicology literally means the study of poisons and their effects on the body, including both legal and illegal drugs. Routine toxicology is often limited to confirming the presence of a few common drugs in blood or urine. The classes of drugs usually identified comprise a group including cocaine, opiates, PCP, benzodiazepines and amphetamines under this heading. As soon as these drugs are taken into the body they are worked on by the liver and kidneys to be eliminated a quickly as possible. Some of the original compound is changed. A challenge for toxicologists is to be able to identify these changed molecules or metabolites as they are termed.

Commercial laboratory suppliers are always perfecting ways to rapidly screen blood and urine for the presence of the common drugs. One of the ways they've come up with is the EMIT test. EMIT stands for Enzyme Multiplied Immunoassay Technique and borrows some of the technology we talked about when we tested for human hemoglobin. The concept of antibodies being made to link up with specific compounds such as drugs is at the core of this technology. Attached to the antibody is an enzyme which causes a color change if the specific drug is present. The test is rapid, sensitive and pretty specific. A few non-illegal drugs have been known to interfere, so the EMIT test is called a screening test and, when positive, must be confirmed by another method.

Confirming the result

We confirm the screening test in body fluids using the same equipment as for a powder or capsule, either by GC or GC/MS, the only difference is how we get a purified sample. A small amount of blood or urine is mixed with chemicals and a layer of solvent. The drugs in the body fluid collect in the solvent layer leaving proteins and biological material behind. The solvent is concentrated by evaporation and a small amount is injected into one of the instruments. The results are compared with standard drug samples previously tested.

All of this is fairly routine in that we generally know which drugs to look for. Of the thousands of drugs that could be prescribed or purchased over the counter, only a handful of illicit drugs are usually tested. Where toxicology really shines is in a medical examiner's case. When a person dies from an overdose, any substance may be involved. Toxicologists must be able to identify anything from aspirin to ancient Chinese herbal remedies not legally obtainable in this country.

When drug abusers die, samples of their liver, urine, blood, brain and sometimes other fluids are sent to the lab for analysis. The tissues are ground up in a homogenizer, a sort of high speed blender. The tissues are then extracted in a similar way to blood and urine. Brain tissue is occasionally analyzed for the presence of inhalants like gasoline or airplane glue. These compounds contain the solvent toluene and are inhaled for sport, sometimes resulting in the sudden death of the abuser. To detect toluene, we use the same gas chromatograph setup we used for fire debris analysis.

Tox results

Richard has no illegal drugs in his blood, but he does have a metabolized form of cocaine in his urine. We got a positive EMIT test and then confirmed the compound benzoylecgonine (benz-oil-EK-oh-neen) by GC/MS. This means he ingested cocaine several hours before his death, his body having had time to remove the drug from his blood and excreted it into his urine. Lisa also has the same substance in her urine, but she has a small amount of the parent drug, cocaine, in her blood. She probably took some cocaine within only a few hours before the murder.

Determining whether a person is "under the influence" of a drug is not as simple as with alcohol. Alcohol is distributed predictably according to the amount of water each organ contains. Cocaine and other drugs do not follow water like alcohol does. There is precious little information about how much cocaine in the blood equates to how much impairment a person shows. Research continues on the effects of various drugs on the operation of a motor vehicle.

BEAUTIFUL and DANGEROUS

Drugs form striking crystals when viewed under polarized light microscopy. The interaction of the molecules with polarized light creates dazzling colors that change according to the orientation of the crystal under observation. Individual crystals form when drugs are mixed with a precipitating chemical like gold chloride (*lower right*). If the mixture is left to dry out, large irregular crystals will grow resulting in the spectacular effects shown here (*top right, next page, facing*).

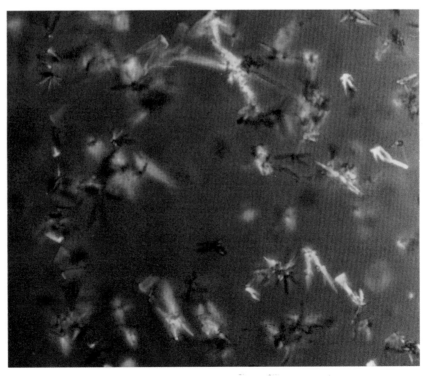

Top: cocaine hydrochloride, below: meth-amphetamine, *next page:* amphetamine, *next page, facing:* methamphetamine.

11

Impressions

HIGH ACTIVITY

One of the busiest sections of the crime lab is the impression evidence section. We like to call it firearms and toolmarks but any evidence that involves one object leaving its mark on another is examined here. The wide assortment of items we look at include shoeprints and tire tracks, scratches on bullets and cartridge cases and marks made by tools. Each mark or impression is compared to objects suspected of having caused them. In Chapter 3 we pointed out the distinction between class and individual characteristics. Nowhere in the crime lab is this distinction more evident than in the impression evidence section.

An object like our crowbar has certain physical characteristics. It has a given width and hardness. When the crowbar is applied to material softer than steel it leaves a mark which gives us clues about its paint, size, hardness and surface. The depth of any scratches left behind and the coarseness of the damage all help us eliminate many items and include this crowbar among others. These are all class characteristics, many other crowbars could have produced the mark but thousands of other tools have been eliminated. When comparing a tool to a mark in an item of evidence the two may be held side by side—never touching—to see if the tool fits. Touching the two, even briefly, might cause a scratch in the evidence that might affect subsequent microscopic analysis.

What it takes

To really succeed in this section of the lab it helps if the criminalist has a varied background. He or she may be an avid shooter, a little bit of a metallurgist or chemist, maybe have a love of mathematics or physics and have an encyclopedic memory for the hundreds of oddly-shaped springs and metal parts found in modern guns. A firearms examiner has to be at once fearless and cautious; we never know the history of a recovered firearm, and test firing it for the first time can be a risky business. For decades the educational requirements for workers in this section were minimal. College was encouraged but not required and police officers were often assigned to this area. Slowly the emphasis has begun to shift. The current feeling is that the principles of ballistics and the application of scientific methods requires a formal education beyond a combination of high school and on-the-job experience. Now, many labs won't even hire a firearms examiner who lacks a college degree. The national group,

AFTE (Association of Firearm and Toolmark Examiners), recommends that workers in this specialty have a college degree.

Soles

One skill that can't be learned at college is the ability to recognize and remember patterns. After staring for hours at a tire track or shoeprint, which at first glance appeared to be an obvious match, we may begin seeing areas where a tread design doesn't quite look like the suspect's tire—or maybe areas where it does. At first and even second glance the two seemed to match perfectly, but after a while we notice little imperfections that prove no similar origin other than brand name. Or the reverse situation. A nick or gouge in the heel area of a print left in the mud at a murder scene may match perfectly with a pair of shoes recovered from a man's closet. Once the similarities are pointed out, everyone can see them, wondering what was so hard about finding them. Being the first to see them in a plaster cast held up next to a photograph of a shoe sole is a task requiring considerable persistence.

Name brands of running shoes are made by factories throughout the Eastern world: Singapore, Malaysia and Taiwan. The brand's style and basic design are similar but each factory makes subtle changes in the tread pattern. Finding these differences can make or break an investigation. We also must take into account such variables as the weight of the person wearing the shoe, the flexibility of the shoe material, how worn the shoes are and the stability of the soil or dust or sand stepped in. How much difference should be expected between the shoe and the print before we deem it an exclusion? Only experience and experimentation can answer that.

We once worked a kidnapping case where we found the suspect's tire tracks at the scene. We began looking at every tire we saw, becoming a little obsessive at times. Parking lots, driveways, anywhere there was a parked car, we'd steal a quick glance at the tires. Fifteen years later we can still clearly picture that tread design. Though we found a few cars with similar tires, we never did find the suspect's vehicle—or the victim. To get a sharp image of a tire track the suspect's tires may be inked and rolled on a long piece of paper, just like a huge fingerprint. When we want a three dimensional look, the tire may be rolled through a long box filled with a mixture of fingerprint powder and cleanser, added to adjust darkness. The resulting track is then photographed. The weight of the vehicle in-

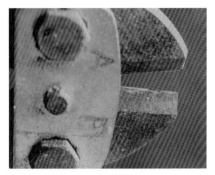

DISTINCTIVE DEFECTS in the way this pair of bolt cutters (*top*) cut through a metal shaft (*above*) can be used to match the tool back to a crime scene.

fluences the shape of the pattern and must be taken into account if a tire has been removed to take impressions.

Compare

The comparison microscope used in the toolmarks section is slightly different from the one used for hairs and fibers. Bullets, wood, and in our case bone and metal, don't pass light well and need to be illuminated from the side. Also, we want to be able to move the light source around making ridges and scratches appear more prominent. This microscope allows large objects to be examined, illumination coming from lights mounted on adjustable arms.

Impressed into poor Richard's skull are marks from the weapon. We'll take a few sections of calvarium (skull) and examine them under the comparison microscope. Bone is rigid but provides an imperfect medium for taking an impression of the crowbar. It acts like a compressed powder and has a crumbly consistency when looked at up close. There are marks, but it doesn't look like we're going to get much detail. In the case of the skull, it is just too pulverized to do us much good.

The window frame is a different story. Being made of a fairly soft metal it provides a good medium for retaining an accurate record of the weapon that struck it. Unfortunately, it wasn't the window frame that died from a beating so it would have been better if we had found matching marks on skull bones. The general curvature of the dent in the window frame conforms well to the outline and circumference of the crowbar. This is an example of a class characteristic. There could be lots of things that have a similar degree of roundness, but there are many more things that have now been excluded. The crowbar is included but not identified by this mark.

A corresponding smudge of silvery substance on the crowbar was previously identified as aluminum when we examined it under the scanning electron microscope. It would be useful if we could individualize these marks, either the one on the crowbar or the window frame. Perhaps there are some tiny scratches left behind in the aluminum frame that exactly correspond to the crowbar. If the crowbar had been used to pry the metal rather than strike it, the comparison would be easier. When an object is simply struck, there may not be many scratches, only direct impressions, kind of like a footprint or tire track.

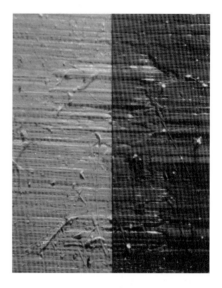

CASTING IMPRESSIONS
To examine the striations of objects like gun barrels that can't be placed under a microscope easily, a cast is made using silicone rubber. The microscopic scratches are reproduced accurately enough to match as if the original object had been viewed. Here, two different colors of silicone rubber are tested for clarity, both halves of the photograph are of casts from the same toolmark made in lead.

Bolt cutters, padlock hasps, wrenches, doorknobs, screwdrivers and anything that might be encountered in a burglary can be mounted under the comparison microscope. It consists of twin low power scopes joined above by a "comparison bridge," a system of lenses and prisms that enable the observer to see two images simultaneously. With a turn of a knob, the view can be changed from split-screen to a "double exposure" where each view overlays the other.

Irreconcilable differences

Using the crowbar, pretending to be the intruder, we see no way to get the smudge of aluminum on the curved end to line up with the dent on the window frame. It seems natural to hold it from the straight end and swing the curved, heavy end towards the window, like a club. If a person tried to swing the hook end through the window, they'd risk getting the hook over the threshold and might have trouble pulling it back. But all of this assumes a person standing outside the window, smashing the glass inward. How does he make contact with the inside lip of the window frame leaving a dent there without also leaving a gouge clear across the bottom part of the whole frame? Answer: He doesn't. He breaks the window from the inside of the bedroom and in so doing, the crowbar crashes through the glass and leaves the mark we see here. This scenario doesn't agree with the witness' account of how the crime occurred, but it fits nicely with the evidence.

We have called the detectives in for a little demonstration. The window frame is set up in approximately the position it was built into the house, and we proceed to pretend to smash the glass, first from one side then the other. It quickly becomes clear that the glass was broken from the inside! The detectives greet this revelation with varying degrees of interest. To some it means they'll have to re-interview Lisa and neighbors from the house facing the window. To others it means the crime lab can't seem to do anything right, and oh, by the way, have you finished the blood typing yet? To us it means the plot just got thicker.

Although no shots were fired at our crime scene, the firearms section of the lab is an integral part of our comprehensive look at a full service crime lab.

ARTIST'S CONCEPTION
A drawing of how a crowbar was used to smash a window helps criminalists understand why the evidence may not agree with witness' accounts. A two-way transfer of evidence occurs when the crowbar leaves paint on the window and takes away glass and aluminum traces.

Firearms identification

When a bullet travels down the length of a gun barrel, the softer lead or copper of the bullet is worn away ever so slightly by the hardened steel of the barrel. Tiny imperfections which were introduced into the rifling of the barrel when it was first manufactured are created in the surface of the bullet. Rifling is the gently twisting groove pattern scribed into a gun barrel to cause the bullet to spin as it leaves the barrel, adding to ballistic stability and accuracy.

There are actually several places where the hard steel of the gun leaves its mark on the softer metal of the ammunition. The bullet is usually made of lead or jacketed with copper, both of which are softer than steel. A cartridge consists of a case containing gunpowder and a primer, topped off by a bullet. We don't appreciate it when someone calls the whole cartridge a "bullet." A gun is really a machine designed to hold on to a small, contained explosion and direct the results in a safe (for the operator at least) and accurate manner. Modern cartridges are fired by a firing pin striking an area which has been loaded with a shock sensitive explosive called a primer. This tiny charge in turn sets off a larger, rapidly burning, amount of gunpowder. A huge amount of pressure builds until the cartridge can no longer hold it, sometimes as high as 50,000 pounds per square inch. The bullet is forced outward, but the cartridge is also

BITS AND PIECES OF METAL are often all a firearms examiner has to work with. Fragments of copper jackets, flattened lead bullets and empty cartridge cases may harbor microscopic damage in the form of scratches left by the hardened steel of a gun. The scratches may be matched back to the one and only gun that fired the ammunition.

forced backward, slamming up against the breechface, a solidly made area of a gun which supports the "head" of the cartridge case. The force is great enough to stamp an impression of the breech into the surface of the cartridge head.

The firing pin also leaves marks on the primer. Still more marks are made by loading and ejecting levers found in semiautomatic firearms which extract the spent shell and fling it away. Just the act of cycling a cartridge through a gun without even firing it can leave permanent scratches in the case that are unique to the gun. When a suspect's gun is examined in the lab, it will be test fired into a box filled with cotton or a tank of water to provide us bullets and cartridges with a known history. Using the comparison microscope the known cartridges and bullets are compared with the ones in question. With patience, skill and a little luck we can definitively say that this firearm and no other fired this bullet, or ejected this cartridge case. One criminalist insists that we point out that the *bullet* is what caused the damage to the victim, not the cartridge case. The cartridge case is used to *associate* a particular firearm to a shooting scene.

The value of luck cannot be overstated. A bullet may leave the muzzle of a gun at over a thousand feet per second and slam into a concrete wall,

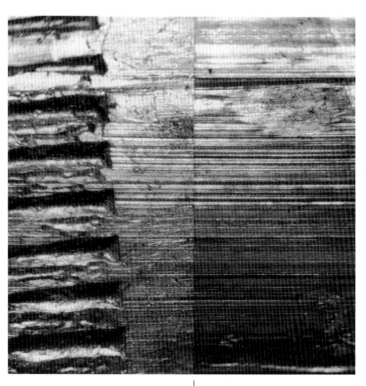

STRIATIONS ON A .41 CALIBER MAGNUM bullet removed at autopsy from a murder victim (*right half*) match the test fired bullet fired through the suspect's own gun (*left half*). The split view is the combination of two microscopes linked optically through a system of prisms. The fine horizontal scratches are the striations, the large gouges are a normal feature on the bullet.

test-fire bullet from
suspect's gun

bullet recovered from
victim's body

deforming it beyond all recognition. Just about anything can and does happen to flying projectiles. Soft lead bullets are notorious for flattening out when they hit hard objects or even when they just hit plain water. Copper jacketed bullets may come loose from their jackets or disintegrate into numerous sharp pieces. In one case, we were photographing the leather jacket of a shooting victim. He'd fallen to the ground where he'd been shot twice more. When we turned the jacket over, we felt something odd. Between the outer shell and inner lining were two flattened lead bullets. They had penetrated his body and the lining of the jacket but didn't have enough energy left to pierce the outer leather. They had remained unseen inside the jacket during the examinations of more than one criminalist.

This gun only

When a bullet or casing is collected from a crime scene we can often assist investigators by observing details about it without waiting for a firearm to be discovered. With a few important exceptions, the direction of twist and number of lands and grooves impressed into the bullet or the nature of the scratches left in a cartridge case can give us an idea of which make of gun might have fired it. Direction of twist refers to the right or left hand spin given the bullet as it leaves the barrel. Grooves are the cuts in the barrel of a gun that form "lands," the term for the metal ridges remaining between the grooves. It's the lands that grip the bullet and give it a twist as it speeds through. Smith & Wesson guns are known for having five lands twisting to the right, Colts for six-left. Unfortunately, there are exceptions to this rule. To determine the direction of twist, we point the bullet away from us and look down from above. The marks on a fired bullet having a right twist will angle to the right as they go from base to nose. Left twist bullets have marks angling to the left. The number of marks around the whole bullet are added up.

When two bullets are placed base to base, we can sometimes tell at a glance if we should be looking for more than one firearm. If the lands don't match up in twist and number, or if the bullets are of different caliber, there's no point in trying to compare them microscopically. Just as with blood typing, exclusions are often quick and definite, matches usually take great effort.

We try to teach our detectives and crime scene technicians the importance of noting such details as which spent cases are in which chambers (in the case of a revolver). Even marking the orientation of how the cartridge case sits in the cylinder can help us get going on a microscopic comparison. We have an extensive library of ammunition, and we know people often mix brands in the same firearm or even reload their own ammo. It's important for us to test-fire the gun using a similar type of ammunition if possible. Some police officers rightly concerned with safety don't hesitate to unload a firearm as soon as they find one at a scene. That's OK with us, but we hope they take a moment and note a few things about its condition. In the case of a revolver they could place a mark on either side of the cylinder before it is opened, then fitting a styrofoam coffee cup over the cartridges will preserve valuable information for the lab while rendering the gun safe to handle.

Side by side

We often make several test fires through an evidence gun and then try to match them under the scope before looking at the evidence bullets. It can happen that sequentially fired bullets don't match each other even though we know we fired them from the same gun. This isn't very common, but can indicate some fouling of the barrel or other transient effect. Another set of test fires usually produces good matches.

To perform a bullet "match," we place a test fired bullet under one lens of the comparison microscope and the questioned bullet, recovered from a body, for example, under another. There must be a significant number of striae (STRY-ah), or scratches, on the surface of the test fired bullet which line up with striae on a questioned bullet. In the sixty-plus years since the techniques were developed, there have been attempts to automate or improve on this procedure, all without success. Slowly we rotate the bullet, measuring the widths of the land impressions made by the gun barrel. Seeing similar striae on both the test fired bullet and the evidence bullet, we decide if the bullets are only similar or really match. Many times the match is a judgement call and we frequently ask another examiner to come over to the scope and have a look, too. In the case of clear, unambiguous matches, two examiners will agree without reservation. It's in the cases that aren't so clear where we earn our salary. How many scratches must line up before it's a match? There's no universally accepted rule. The thing that keeps us sharp, though, is knowing that our work will most certainly be challenged if our results have any impact on the case at all.

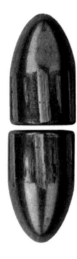

BASE TO BASE, these two 9mm bullets show a similar left twist and number of lands. The twist direction is determined by observing how the land impressions angle towards the left from base to nose.

There is some controversy about photographing firearm and toolmark matches. Without taking sides, it is interesting to note that bullets are three dimensional objects and photographs are not. Anyone looking at the photo must be aware that striae that don't seem to line up, especially at the edges of the photo, might look differently under a microscope. What should a criminalist do when his or her boss orders a photograph of the bullet match even if the criminalist strongly feels that it would be misleading to anyone looking at the photo? Should we just believe the criminalist when he or she says it was a match and leave it at that?

All's well

Another task is determining the functionality of a firearm involved in a crime. A common defense argument involves a claim of accidental discharge, where a pistol was fired unintentionally, perhaps it has a so-called hair trigger. We routinely check a firearm's trigger pull by mounting it to a bench and slowly increasing a weight attached to the trigger until the (unloaded) firearm snaps its hammer. For example, it's a tough sell for a defendant to assert that his semiautomatic pistol with a twelve-pound trigger pull went off accidentally.

In addition to trigger pull, we often must check the firearm for unusual operation. In one case, a man claimed he and a friend were sitting on a bed looking at his .44 caliber magnum single action revolver. A single action pistol requires the hammer to be cocked before the gun can be fired. This fellow said he accidentally dropped the pistol on the floor where it went off, sending a bullet into his friend's chest, killing him.

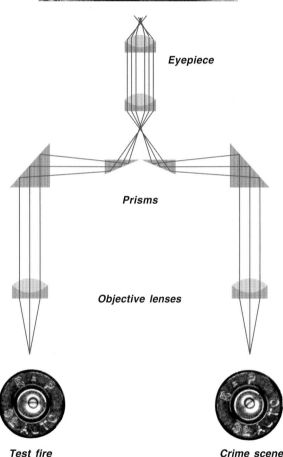

Test fire   Crime scene

A COMPLEX SYSTEM OF PRISMS and lenses allow two separate images from two microscopes to be compared side-by-side. In this example, the firing pin impressions are under analysis. High-pressures in a firearm cause the casing to become "stamped" with fine machine markings in the breechface of the gun. These markings are unique and reproducible.

The trajectory of the wound in the victim was consistent with the story, travelling upward from below. We didn't think this gun could go off like that, however, so we performed a simple experiment. We prepared a safe cartridge by pulling the bullet and dumping out the gunpowder leaving only the primer intact. We loaded this into the revolver so that the cartridge was under the hammer. The gun was not cocked. Holding the gun by the grips upside down, with the hammer down and the barrel up, we struck the hammer on a phone book (to protect the gun from damage). Sure enough, the primer went off with a loud pop. It seems that the firing pin was just able to contact the primer of the cartridge without even the trigger being pulled. No charges were filed against the man.

HELD STEADY FOR TESTING this pistol is locked into a machine rest. During a test firing the recoil will rotate the pistol up but it can be returned to the original pre-firing position.

Another functionality test that's kind of fun is the determination of full-auto capability. Federal and state firearm laws prohibit the possession of firearms that can fire twice or more for each squeeze of the trigger. Several models of so-called assault rifles are available for sale after they have been converted to semiautomatic action. These are legal as long as they haven't been modified back to their original full-auto status. A growing number of these firearms have been declared illegal in our state regardless of their automatic status. It's up to us to see if a suspect's firearm falls within a list of outlawed guns.

Some of the guns we get to test are quite exotic including the Israeli UZI, the communist bloc AK-47, the American MAC-10 and MAC-11, Heckler and Koch and the good old military-issued M16. Most of these have been modified to only fire once for each pull of the trigger, but we have to drag ourselves out to the range and test fire them to be certain.

An unusual item we occasionally see are homemade silencers. The legal definition of a silencer includes devices attached to a gun with the intent to reduce a loud report, however slightly. What we receive at the lab, though, are weird attempts to duplicate the James Bond type of a silencer made popular by movies and TV shows. None of them works well at all. Especially in the case of a revolver, much of the noise of a discharge comes out the sides of the gun as well as out the barrel. In addition, a bullet travelling faster than the speed of sound, about 1,100 feet per second, will make a sharp crack from the sonic boom of the bullet. The only way to quiet the bullet down is to slow it to below the speed of sound.

The fatigue of staring into the comparison scope for hours on end is compensated by the variety of activities we get perform in the firearms section. One such activity involves establishing muzzle to target distance. Central to many defense theories is the claim that the defendant was standing a specified distance from the victim. Perhaps the defendant was fearful of being stabbed and shot the victim in self defense. Perhaps the story has the defendant accidentally firing the firearm from across the street, never intending to hurt the victim. If we can establish how far away the shooter was from the victim, we will have added lots of good information to the search for the truth.

When a gun is fired, numerous grains of hot, burned and unburned powder come flying out of the barrel along with the bullet. These particles spray outward in an ever widening cone of debris that lack the energy to travel very far. In fact, the particles are so light that after only a few feet, they've fallen to the earth. If a person is shot at close range, hot gases and powder particles blast their way into the skin and or clothing forming a sort of macabre tattoo around the bullet hole. The diameter of this tattoo depends on the firearm, the ammunition and the distance from the end of the barrel (muzzle) to the bullet hole. At the police shooting range we'll set up a piece of paper or clothing and shoot at it from various distances. We'll try to use the original gun and same type of ammo used by the shooter.

Some bullet wounds bleed profusely covering up powder patterns on clothing. We discovered that viewing the clothes in total darkness through an inexpensive infrared viewer, similar to a night vision scope, makes the blood invisible and allows us to see the gunpowder pattern if there is one.

Restorative powers

Guns have a serial number stamped into their frames when they are manufactured, allowing us to trace their ownership. In our state, it is a crime to remove this serial number or to possess a firearm that has had its serial number obliterated. If we can restore the number we might find the original owner or trace the firearm as it was sold from one person to another. The duty of restoring defaced numbers usually falls to the firearms examiner, although it's really accomplished through chemistry and a bit of metallurgy.

SERIAL NUMBERS STAMPED into metal like those in the pistol frame above leave lasting impressions even after they have been ground into obscurity.

The stamping process involves a steel punch in the shape of a numeral being hammered into the metal frame of a gun, bicycle or automobile engine block. The force of the punch actually compresses the molecules of the metal a bit deeper than the numeral itself. If a criminal gouges, grinds or scrapes the numerals off we can usually restore the number by finishing the job for him. We grind, sand and finally polish the metal to a level just deeper than the deepest gouge. We strive for a mirror finish. It seems impossible, because now we have even less to work with than the criminal left us. Where there was a damaged serial number, we now have a thin strip of polished metal.

Slowly we apply a solution of acid and copper salts to the mirror. Presently, the number is revealed in a ghostlike fashion. We'd better hurry and photograph it, the numbers often fade within minutes. Sometimes the numbers appear very clear, other times we must guess at a few digits. The reason it works is that the compressed metal etches more slowly than the uncompressed metal, allowing a slight contrast between the two until the acid catches up. As long as there is a contrast, we can read the number.

Residuals

The cloud of gas and hot particles blowing out of a gun as it fires contains residue from the primer chemicals as well. This residue can collect on the clothes and skin of the person shooting. The gunshot residue, or GSR, can be identified by its unusual combination of elements lead, barium and antimony. These metals are identified by the elemental analysis feature in the scanning electron microscope. Some agencies have discontinued the testing for GSR, thinking that there are too many false positives to make the test reliable. They point out that merely handling a gun or standing next to a gun while it is fired can lead to GSR being detected. We don't abandon a test just because it might lead to erroneous conclusions. Scientific testing is not an all-or-nothing affair; the results must be carefully interpreted. Yes, there are many ways to get GSR on clothing without having fired a gun. Let's look at the big picture and find out how much GSR is present, compared to how much is found on other suspects. Is there more on the right hand of a right-handed suspect? Is there some in a nasal swab? Is there less on the suspect's accomplice? New formulations of primer chemicals eliminate lead and other metals entirely. The impact of these new compounds on the future of GSR testing is uncertain.

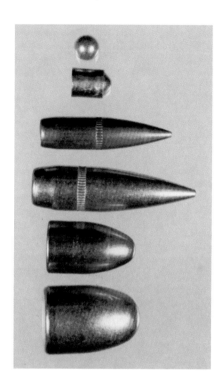

AN ASSORTMENT of projectiles examined by the firearms section of the crime lab. *From top:* .173 cal. copper plated BB, .20 cal. pellet, 5.56mm cal. full metal jacket, 7.62mm cal. NATO, 9mm cal. round nose and .45 cal. round nose. These bullets have been pulled and not fired, note the lack of land impressions.

A vision of the future

One serious problem facing firearms examiners is the serial shooting. A gun continues to manufacture evidence every time it is fired and may be carried long distances before it is used again. If a gun is used in California and later in Oklahoma, how can we in California know about the evidence recovered in the other state? Crime labs can't afford to operate in isolation and must have a way of sharing information about microscopic examinations. Medical doctors have had a way of doing this for many years. Many hospitals have video conferencing where printouts of EKG strips and X-rays can be captured by a digital camera and shared with other hospitals anywhere in the world. Why not crime labs, too?

Evidence on-line

The fingerprint and now DNA databases have become among the most powerful weapons in the law enforcement arsenal. Not to be outdone, firearms identification specialists have come up with versions of their own. Both the FBI and the ATF (Bureau of Alcohol, Tobacco and Firearms) have deployed computerized systems that store images of bullets, cartridge cases and related information. When local crime labs have a shooting case they can capture a digital image of a bullet or cartridge case and compare it with data already entered by the federal agencies or other crime labs who are on-line. The FBI's system is called DRUGFIRE, so named to attack the gun-related violence associated with drug trafficking. The ATF has a pair of similar programs called BULLETPROOF for bullet images and BRASSCATCHER for cartridge case information. Future plans call for the two systems to be fully integrated to allow information to be shared between all agencies having the necessary computerized hardware.

DRUGFIRE

In only a few years over 65,000 cases have been entered into the DRUGFIRE database. The data entry is the result of the hard work of numerous examiners and technicians in hundreds of local crime labs. The system has already proved its usefulness in over 2,500 cases where "hits" or links to other cases have been made in the same or different states, cities and jurisdictions. Previously unrelated cases, they have now been discovered to be linked by firearms evidence.

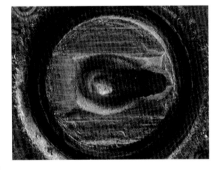

DRUGFIRE
An example of a DRUGFIRE cartridge case image. The image was captured by a laboratory in another county and loaded onto the database. When a search is conducted many cartridge cases from different labs are available for review. The image is of a cartridge case primer discharged in a Glock .40 caliber pistol.

SPENT BUT NOT USELESS
On a .32 caliber cartridge case the letters on the headstamp identify the manufacturer, in this instance Remington-Peters. *Below:* Side view of the item. Scratches left by the extractor and ejector as well as other parts of the gun can be matched to the exact firearm which ejected this cartridge case.

It works like this: A firearm recovered from a suspect is test fired in the lab. The fired cartridge case is mounted under a video camera attached to a powerful Sun (Sun Microsystems) computer. The lighting is adjusted and—*click*—a digital "target" image is captured. After the target image is captured, the computer program identifies distinguishing marks on the image and reduces them to numeric values. This data is searched against tens of thousands of images stored in regional databases from over a hundred labs across the country. The list of labs contributing images is growing constantly. Each lab is linked by high-speed phone connection with other DRUGFIRE lab's computers and download images from one lab to another. The results of a search may include hundreds of candidates, displayed twenty-four at a time on the screen. The target image from our lab is displayed in the center of the screen. If we want a closer look we just click the mouse on one of the images. Just as in the comparison microscope, the two images can be placed side by side, moved or rotated to allow overlaying of the images. The split screen or center line may be swept across the image to look for areas of similarity. Unlike the comparison microscope, the new test fire image can be instantly shared with another lab anywhere in the DRUGFIRE world.

In the example printed here we have specified a ".40 caliber cartridge case with an elliptical shaped firing pin impression." Within seconds a search returns two dozen images matching our requirements displayed on screen in a small "thumbnail" version. Hundreds more await viewing when we're done with the first two-dozen. We can easily spot the characteristic firing pin impressions typical of Glock-made guns. The overall shape of the firing pin impression can be a clue as well. In our Glock example, the shape of the firing pin isn't actually round, but oval, another peculiarity.

In addition to this example, other marks on cartridge cases are catalogued in DRUGFIRE. Ejector, extractor and chamber marks are also being imaged into the database. Chamber marks form in the cartridge case as it expands upon discharge. Even images of bullets are being entered, although not as quickly as cartridge case images. Bullets are often damaged and as a result require much more human manipulation than the more consistently reproducible marks on cartridge cases.

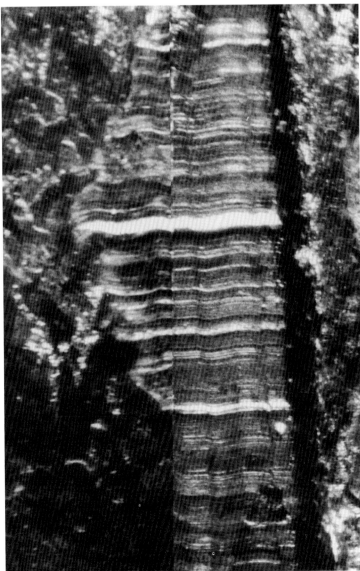

TINY IMPERFECTIONS in the metal jaws of these pliers left telltale marks in brass doorknobs twisted open by a burglar. At right is the view under the comparison microscope. The photo is split in two halves, left and right. On the left is the mark from a brass doorknob recovered from the crime scene. On the right is a test scratch made in a sheet of lead at the crime lab.

The width of the pliers' jaws is an example of a class characteristic, individual characteristics are seen in the microscopic scratches. The good agreement of individual characteristics between the pliers and the doorknob conclusively identifies this pair of pliers as the tool used.

12

Credibility

Not exactly Perry Mason

Courtroom drama portrayed on television shows is usually far from reality. The introduction of cameras in real courtrooms has forced screenwriters to depict trials much more accurately as audiences become more sophisticated. The only way to get the flavor of what really happens is to actually testify in court. The next best thing is to be there to hear and see the testimony being offered. Since we can't do either of those things in a book, we'll have to settle for third best, actually the worst, reading other people's testimony from a transcript.

The following transcript is an actual excerpt from a trial involving three defendants accused of manufacturing methamphetamine in their small house. All three were convicted so the names were changed to protect the guilty.

JOHN Q. CRIMINALIST, called as a witness by and on behalf of the People, having been first duly sworn, and examined and testified as follows:

THE CLERK: You do solemnly swear that the testimony you may give in the matter now pending before this court shall be the truth, the whole truth and nothing but the truth, so help you God?

THE WITNESS: I do.

THE CLERK: Please be seated. State your full name spell your last name for the record.
THE WITNESS: John Q. C-R-I-M-I-N-A-L-I-S-T

DIRECT EXAMINATION BY MR. TERRY:

Q. Mr. Criminalist, where are you employed?
A. At the County Sheriff's Crime Laboratory

Q. What's your position with the crime laboratory?
A. I'm employed as a criminalist.

Q. Do you have any special training or experience to qualify you to be a criminalist?
A. In 1979, I received my bachelor of science degree in microbiology. This included courses in organic chemistry, general chemistry, biochemistry and quantitative analysis. For a little over one year, I was employed by the Department of Justice Crime Laboratory, and after that at County Sheriff's Department.

Q. Mr. Criminalist, on the 13th of June, did you have occasion to respond to a residence at 6534 Katy Street in the City of Simi Valley?

A. Yes, I did.

Q. Approximately what time of the day was it that you arrived?

A. Approximately 1 o'clock in the morning.

Q. Now, when you went to the location on Katy Street what was your assignment at that time?

A. To first attempt to identify what, if any, synthesis was being done at that location and then to attempt to stop it or at least control it so that it would not get out of control and cause a fire, for example. And second, to collect and catalog any evidence that may have been pointed out to me.

Q. Now, what did you do to try and make a determination as to what type of chemical reaction was going on at the location?

A. Immediately after being informed by the police that it was secure, we observed the reaction through the door and identified at least the scale of operation. Then an officer, I can't remember who, presented me with a piece of paper that had a reaction synthesis on it. And this we determined to be a particular reaction and gave us an idea as to what might possibly be being done at that location.

Q. Now, where was this piece of paper given to you?

A. At the back door of the residence.

Q. Was it brought from inside the residence to your location outside the residence?

A. I don't believe so. I believe it was part of an earlier arrest perhaps; and it was just shown to me by an officer who was outside the residence.

Q. I'm going to show you an exhibit that's previously been marked as People's Exhibit No. 2. Inside this particular exhibit are a number of papers. I would ask if you would take a look at these. There are quite a few of them. So it may take a while.

Just so you know, basically, what I'm asking you to look at. There are preprinted objects that appear to be like printed by press or typewriter. And then there are some handwritten objects. I 'm merely really asking you to look at the handwritten stuff.

A. Very well.

Q. Now, have you had the opportunity look at the items contained in there?

A. Yes, I have.

Q. The handwritten items, can you tell basically what — how would you categorize those handwritten items?

A. They seem to be of a different character. Some seem to be poetry, others appear to be chemical references, some appear to be lists of chemicals and, finally, others appear to be recipes.

Q. Now, of those recipes that you see there could you make a determination from your background and training what type of chemicals are attempting to be made by those recipes?

A. Yes.

Q. What type of substances are attempted to be made by those recipes?

MR. HOWARD: Your Honor, may I — I don't know if we have a proper foundation for his opinion. We haven't heard a list or any of the chemicals yet.

THE COURT: Well, I don't believe that it is necessary to get a list of chemicals before you can interpret a formula or a recipe. I didn't understand that the list was a part of a formula. I understand there are lists and there are recipes. Are you suggesting that the list of chemicals is a part of: the recipe, Mr. Howard?

MR. HOWARD: Well, I'm understanding that the recipe consists of chemicals which, put in certain proportions, will —It will result in another chemical or some kind of an end-result product. And I haven't heard any foundational basis from which this individual can make such assumption unless he' just reading off — just reading off a list and it doesn't take any expertise to read a list of ingredients from which a recipe is derived.

THE COURT: It might need clarification. Are you reading a chemical formula, you're asked to determine what it is a recipe for?

THE WITNESS: No, actually not. It seems to be a list of steps to follow, and it does not indicate any final product.

THE COURT: I see. Are there specific chemicals listed?

THE WITNESS: Yes, there are.

THE COURT: Well, can you list the chemicals before you render your opinion?

THE WITNESS: How shall I refer to this particular hand written document ?

THE COURT: You want to just read off what the steps are, if it's not too long? And then you can make your opinion about what the cook is supposed to make out of this recipe without spoiling the broth.

THE WITNESS: Very well. Appears to be the fifth page of the blue binder.

Step A is to measure out 100 milliliters of methanol. Add an eighth of a teaspoon of mercuric chloride crystals and stir until dissolved.

Step B. Place 50 grams of aluminum foil to a flask. Next pour the methanol in a flask; and slosh around until foil is wet.

Step C. Add 300 milliliters of ether to the flask and shake. Next place the flask in ice chest with ice and water.

*   *   *

(A few key steps are deleted in the interest of public safety)

Step 2, Section A: Prepare a saltwater solution, one quart distilled water and one quarter pound of salt. And then add 300 milliliters of ether. Now add this solution to flask. Step B. Let sit for another eight hours in ice chest. It's my opinion that if carried out, these steps would result in the production of methamphetamine.

MR. TERRY: Now, you may go ahead and place those items back in the black case, please.

Q. Mr. Criminalist, you mentioned that you initially were to make a determination from the items that you saw inside as to what type of reactions were occurring in the house; is that a fair summary?

A. Yes.

Q. What did you do in that regard upon your entry?

A. There was some concern as to whether PCP was being manufactured. So we looked and entered the residence to examine the reaction and, basically, to eliminate or confirm the possibility of PCP being manufactured.

Q. What was the result of your initial observation?

A. We weren't sure until we received that piece of paper that was presented to us by that officer.

Q. And how did that help in your evaluation?

A. It fit the whole picture. It gave a formula in chemical symbols. Not the formula I just read, but in chemical shorthand it showed the method for production of methamphetamine.

Using that, we began to identify the other parts of the reaction, the sizes of the flasks, the solvents that were present, for example. And using those two pieces of information, what we observed and what we were shown on the piece of paper tended to support this idea that methamphetamine was being manufactured.

Q. Now, one of the substances you talked about in that formula was P2P. What is P2P?

A. Actually, throughout the written records here we find only P2 mentioned. However, it appears that that's synonymous with P2P.

Q. What is P2P?

A. P2P is short for phenyl-2-propanone.

Q. You also read as to one of the ingredients in that particular list as being methylamine. Is that a correct pronunciation of it?

A. Yes, it is.

Q. Is that also a precursor for methamphetamine?

A. Yes, it is.

Q. Did you look at the items that were in the house at that point to make a determination as to whether those substances were present?

A. I believe we waited until the search warrant was delivered.

Q. How long was that?

A. I believe it arrived around seven a.m.

Q. So we're talking about five to six hours later?

A. Yes.

Q. What did you do during that five or six-hour period, from the time of your initial entry to the time the search warrant arrived?

A. We made sure that all of the flammable and explosive chemicals were well away from the house. We waited and we read literature, which showed various syntheses that the government — let's see, Drug Enforcement Agency publishes to further try to characterize this reaction. And I believe we walked through the house a few times as well.

Q. Now, when you say you got the flammables away from the house, what do you mean by that?

A. There were several large cans marked ether and acetone and so we physically took them out of the house and put them in the backyard.

Q. Are these flammable fluids?
A. Yes, they are.

Q. Now, after the search warrant arrived, what did you do in your investigation?
A. We systematically went through the house and examined all bottles and containers, recorded their contents — in other words, if they were approximately half full or a quarter full. We then took samples of each of them or we took the entire container if the sample was very small.

Q. Did you seize certain items that you transported back to the crime laboratory for later analysis?
A. Yes, I did.

Q. Did you see items that you later determined contained methylamine?
A. Yes, I did.

Q. Can you describe for the Court what the item looked like that you seized that contained methylamine? And how much methylamine did you determine there was present?
A. May I consult my notes ?

Q. If it will help to refresh your recollection.
A. We discovered two glass bottles approximately one gallon size each. First one was half full of liquid. Second one was approximately four-fifths full of liquid and we analyzed one of them to contain methylamine. The other one was not analyzed at this time.

Q. Did you find any objects in the house that contained P2P or phenyl-2-propanone?
A. We found two glass bottles, which were hand-labeled P2 — excuse me. They were labeled P2P. They are approximately one pint each. However, the liquid contained in each one was only approximately two milliliters. One of them contained phenyl-2-propanone or P2P. The other one did not.

Q. Now, were there substances also contained within the house that you took back and later tested and determined that they contained methamphetamine?

A. Yes.

Q. Can you describe what those containers looked like and the quantity of the substance that you determined to be possessed in those?

A. Okay. First one was a bottled water bottle, approximately five gallon size, approximately half full of a brownish liquid, which contained methamphetamine.

Another seizure was two clear plastic baggies of brownish powder. First plastic baggie contained 23.8 grams of: approximately four percent methamphetamine.

Second plastic baggie contained 13.48 grams of methamphetamine. The quantity was not determined, since the similarity to the other powder was very much evident.

Q. Did you see any other items that contained methamphetamine?

A. Also — Yeah. The glass-reaction vessel, which was 22 liter size, approximately half full of liquid, was found to contain methamphetamine.

Q. On any of the items that you seized, did you seize the paperwork also that was within that laboratory at all?

A. No we did not.

MR. TERRY: I don't believe I have any other questions, Mr. Criminalist.

THE COURT: Cross-examination.

MR. CHARLES: Thank you.

CROSS-EXAMINATION BY MR. CHARLES:

Q. Mr. Criminalist, you said that you, at some time after the policemen went in, walked through the house, you said, several times; is that correct?
A. That's correct.

Q. Do you have any idea how many times you walked through the house?
A. More than three and less than seven,

Q. Okay. Do you recall seeing at any time any woman's clothing or girl's clothing?

A. I do not.

Q. Did you ever at any time see anything that indicated a woman was living in that house?
A. I don't recall.

MR. CHARLES: All right. Thank you. I have nothing further, your Honor.

THE COURT: Mr. Howard.

CROSS- EXAMINATION BY MR HOWARD:

Q. Mr. Criminalist, as to the possession of Methylamine —is that how you —
A. Methylamine.

Q. — Methylamine, you found two glass bottles of it is that correct? One was half full, one was four-fifths full?
A. We found two glass bottles that smelled like ammonia. Only one was analyzed, and it was found to contain methylamine.

Q. Do you recall now which one, whether it was the one that was half full or the one that was four-fifths full?
A. I don't know. I've looked in the notes and I don't see.

Q. Was there a qualitative amount you were able to discern from the analysis? What percentage — or does that apply with this chemical?
A. Yes, it does. I did not perform one however. I have an opinion as to the approximate purity of it in that it commercially can only be prepared to less than 50 percent, closer to 30 percent pure.
It's dissolved in water, and we found this to be dissolved in water. And then we purify the methylamine with a simple chemical extraction. So I would estimate it would also be less than 50 percent.

Q. And these were one gallon — or the bottle that was analyzed was a one-gallon bottle?
A. Yes, that's correct.

Q. Okay. Now, as to the P2P. You ended up actually only finding in one pint-size bottle two milliliters that you could identify as P2P, is that correct?
A. That is correct.

Q. Now, what about a qualitative percentage on that chemical?

A. I can only say that it was not pure. I could not even hazard a guess as to an approximate percentage. Something less than 100 percent.

Q. The methamphetamine — There was a bottled water bottle that was half full, you said, containing methamphetamine?

A. That's correct.

Q. That was in liquid form?

A. Yes, it was.

Q. Did you come up with a qualitative percentage on that?

A. Only an estimate.

Q. And would that be the same estimate as with the other methamphetamines that you found in the powder?

A. It appeared to be, yes.

Q. That being four percent pure?

A. Approximately, uh-huh.

Q. In the recipe that you read earlier, I think you indicated that it was your opinion that the chemicals in the process you read from the piece of paper that you were looking at was a chemical formula for making methamphetamines, is that right?

A. Wasn't really a formula, more a sequence of steps which, if followed, could result in the manufacture of methamphetamine, yes.

Q. Was the inclusion of P2P in these steps that you read?

A. Yes.

Q. Okay. I didn't write it down when you were going through it. Can you tell me based on your memory or from the piece of paper that you looked at earlier the amount of P2P that was necessary, either based on your own experience or based on the list that you wrote— that you read from to manufacture any quantity of methamphetamines?

A. From my recollection I recall it being approximately equal volumes with the methylamine. Certainly depends on how much final product you're looking for, tons or ounces.

Q. Two milliliters of P2P, is that a large enough quantity to make any amount of methamphetamine?

A. Yes.

MR. HOWARD: Okay. Thank you.

THE COURT: Mr. Getty?

CROSS-EXAMINATION BY MR. GETTY:

Q. If you had a half a gallon of methylamine, about how much P2P would it take to turn that all into methamphetamine?

A. Are we assuming approximately 40 percent methylamine?

Q. Approximately the same concentration that you observed.

A. Well, assuming it's approximately 40 percent, then — Did you ask — I'm sorry. How much methamphetamine, then, could you make or how much P2P could you make?

Q. How much P2P would you need to make methamphetamine out of the whole mess?

A. Approximately the same amount of methylamine. If you suggested a half a gallon then I would suggest a half a gallon. That's not exactly right. I'd have to work out the mathematics to find out exactly.

Q. And if you had two milliliters of P2P, how much methamphetamine could you conceivably manufacture?

A. Depending on the purity of the P2P — We'll assume it's completely pure. You could manufacture a gram, perhaps, if you were extremely proficient.

Q. When you say that the brownish powder in the plastic bags was four percent methamphetamine, do I gather, then, that if you wanted to find out now much pure methamphetamine there was in there, that we take four percent of 23.89 grams in one case and 13.48 grams in another?

A. Exactly.

Q. Was the 13.48 gram baggie tested at all?

A. It was tested to the extent that it was identified and confirmed as containing methamphetamine.

Q. Where were these two baggies found?

A. I believe in the same room that the synthesis was taking place, as I recall, they were rolled up and in plain sight on a makeshift table in that room.

Q. Would that be the living room of the residence?

A. I don't believe so. It had the sink and a refrigerator in that room.

Q. It appeared to be a kitchen?
A. Appeared to be.

Q. Prior to your entry, after the police had secured the residence, did you have any conversations with Detective Davis concerning what was going on in the residence?
A. I believe so.

Q. Did you advise him or give him your opinion as to anything that was going on in this residence?
A. I don't believe so, no.

MR. GETTY: I have nothing further.

THE COURT: Mr. TERRY?

REDIRECT EXAMINATION BY MR TERRY:

Q. I don't know if I asked you this earlier. I'm sure someone will remind me if I have. Do you have an opinion as to what the persons were doing inside that particular building with those properties that you seized?
A. I believe that they were synthesizing methamphetamine.

* * *

The drug manufacturing case was rather complex, involving nearly a hundred items of evidence and three defendants, translating into three defense attorneys and one prosecutor. Fortunately for the witnesses, lawyers are generally not allowed to fire questions randomly, each one must take his or her turn then pass the witness to the next attorney. It may not make for thrilling courtroom drama, but this excerpt is truly representative of a typical court experience for a criminalist. If it seems dull to read imagine how jurors must feel, being forced to listen to hours of similar dialog over the course of several days, even weeks? As sworn witnesses, our hearts may pound with anticipation of the next question, but trials aren't held for our entertainment. We are there to explain complex crime lab findings in an understandable way to judges and juries who have weighty decisions to make.

What have we learned

Before we can testify in the matter of People v. Ralph P. we should review our findings and conclusions. We'll make some notes and summarize what we've learned so far.

Blood stains. The blood spatters and stains in the house are consistent with two blood spatter events. A blood spatter event is when liquid blood is put into motion by some mechanical process, such as striking a bloody object. The spatter patterns support a theory that Richard was beaten not less than three times (once to open the skin wound). The blood spatter events occurred at a point approximately where his head was resting, on the sofa where he was found.

Prints. The bloody print on the doorjamb is Lisa's partial palm print in Lisa's own blood. Lisa was found with a wounded wrist that could account for the bloody print. We can't say when the print was made.

Fire Extinguisher. Traces of ammonium phosphate were identified on Ralph's shoes, Richard's shoes and the sofa and carpet in the living room. This substance was similar to the chemical identified in a fire extinguisher discovered under the kitchen sink at the crime scene. The powder was on the surface of bloodstains, not mixed with blood, suggesting blood had already been deposited on the shoes before the extinguisher was discharged. Ralph's and Lisa's fingerprints were also identified on the extinguisher. The fire extinguisher from the kitchen or another one containing ammonium phosphate was discharged at or near the location of the body. It cannot be determined how long after the blood dried on Ralph's shoes the ammonium phosphate powder was transferred. The powder on the shoes of both individuals is similar to the powder from the carpet and sofa and extinguisher but a conclusive match is not possible.

Sexual assault. Weak acid phosphatase and few sperm cells were found on the vaginal samples from Lisa. Assuming a normal volume of ejaculate, this is consistent with a past sexual intercourse, not a recent one. ABO blood grouping is probably not possible and DNA typing may not yield conclusive results because of the small amount of semen present. PCR techniques may be able to amplify enough male DNA to allow typing.

Fire debris. Although what appeared as a distinct burn, or halo, pattern was observed on the carpet, no ignitable liquids were identified in the burned or unburned areas sampled from the crime scene. Highly volatile substances including alcohol or acetone cannot be excluded as having been present.

Blood. Human blood of similar ABO and DNA type to that of Richard was identified on Ralph's shoe and the curved end of the crowbar. Approximately one percent of the Caucasian population would be expected to share the same DNA and ABO types that were identified in the blood on Ralph's shoes. These numbers may change dramatically as we apply population data of different racial groups to the results of blood testing. This blood was in the form of a spatter pattern where the drop has a toe-towards-heel directionality. This shoe was near the source of Richard's liquid blood and was pointed toward the source when the blood spatter event occurred.

Trace evidence. Paint chips of similar color and chemically indistinguishable to paint on Richard's skull were identified on the crowbar. Glass of similar refractive index to that of the bedroom window was embedded in the crowbar. Aluminum metal was identified on the crowbar. Paint similar in color and composition to paint on the crowbar was located on the dent in the window frame. The crowbar was probably used to smash the bedroom window resulting in the transfers of aluminum and glass from the window to the crowbar and paint from the crowbar to the frame. The crowbar was used to strike Richard in the head resulting in a transfer of blood to the crowbar and paint from the crowbar to the victim's skull.

No glass fragments were recovered from Ralph's shoes. Glass fragments similar in refractive index to the bedroom window were identified clinging to Lisa's bathrobe. Lisa's bathrobe could have been near the window when it was broken, or she could have picked up glass particles by touching an area contaminated with glass from the broken window.

Scene reconstruction. A dent in the aluminum window frame corresponded to the crowbar's general shape, but it could not be duplicated in laboratory simulations by striking the window from the outside. The dent could be made easily by the crowbar striking the frame from inside the house.

The electrical cord is similar to cord used in a bedroom lamp and could have come from it. A circular pattern of dust disturbance was observed on the top of the dresser. Disturbances in the dust on top of the bedroom dresser agree with the dimensions of the lamp and indicate that the lamp was probably on the dresser at one time.

There are many more observations we could record and interpret including our discovery of cocaine and marijuana residue, the results of blood alcohol and toxicology testing and the identification of pet hairs and carpet fibers. Depending on the prosecutor's original requests, we may or may not exhaustively list every item examined and what was found. In our state, the defense is entitled to a copy of our actual lab notes, a practice that horrifies some criminalists in other states. Because of this rule, called mutual discovery, we can be assured that any details we fail to mention in our report to the DA will be noticed and requested by the defense.

So shall it be written

Besides testifying, writing a clear, understandable report is, probably our most challenging and important task. No matter how dazzling our scientific procedure, if our reports are muddy and confused or reach conclusions not based upon what we actually examined, they'll assist no one. Most of the reports we write will speak for us in courts of law, and we often won't have to testify about our findings if our written report is clear and the findings are not disputed. Many of our conclusions are not argued by either side even though they are essential to proving the elements of the alleged crime. Both attorneys might agree that a certain white powder was cocaine, for example, and have no wish to belabor the point. The lab report is frequently introduced into evidence in lieu of our sworn testimony. Some jurisdictions even make us swear an oath on the pages of the report itself.

The district attorney may prepare a stipulation, or agreement, which is offered to defense counsel. After the wording of the agreement is haggled over, the DA may address the judge and announce for the record something like, "Bob Smith, a criminalist with Smalltown crime laboratory, is deemed to have testified that he found cocaine in People's Exhibit number one . . . ." This agreement saves everyone a considerable amount of time. Cooling our heels outside court, waiting to testify takes us away from examining evidence and can easily consume a good portion of a day. The more well known we are among the attorneys and the better our reputation, the more likely our testimony will be stipulated. It is the defendant's right not to stipulate anything, however, and we could be called to testify on every single case we touch. There would not be time for much else. The drug analysis criminalists alone easily generate a hundred subpoenas each per month in a moderate-sized laboratory.

On occasion the district attorney will not wish to ask the defense to stipulate our findings. It may be part of the trial strategy that our in-person testimony will have greater impact than just a reading of a report into the record. The flip side is when the defense wants to take its shot at diminishing our findings by cross-examining us. In that case they won't agree to any stipulation offered by the DA regarding our testimony.

Weasel words

When the chemical map for semen is negative, we might be tempted to report that there is no semen on the sheet. A more correct phrase is "no semen was detected on the sheet." We have resorted to the carefully chosen words "none detected" or "not found" rather than "not present" to cover the limits of our testing. We have mentioned how we sometimes seem to hide behind vague sounding terms in our reports. Matches are rare and, when we see them, writing a report is easy: *This bullet was fired from this gun.* Exclusions are equally straightforward: *This subject could not have contributed that semen stain.* It's when, as one criminalist put it, the evidence "mumbles" that we have to equivocate. "More likely than not," "could have come from," "may have come from," "probably came from," and, "is consistent with," are each phrases we use in trying to express our varying degrees of confidence with respect to a comparison that we've made.

Ralph wants to plead guilty. Word has come from the district attorney that he admits to the whole thing. He did the crime and wants to do the time.

Ralph admits breaking in through the bedroom window, tying up Lisa, raping her, waiting for Richard, and clobbering him to death with the crowbar he got from Richard's garage. He claims he washed it off at the sink and dried it with the bloody towel we found. He says he set the fire in the living room with rubbing alcohol. Then he got scared and put it out with the fire extinguisher. The extinguisher was practically dead, but it did have enough powder to knock back the flames for him to stamp out. He says he did it because he loves Lisa and wanted Richard to divorce her, something Richard was apparently disinclined to do.

We're glad that's settled. Now, where did we put the evidence for that new case which was just assigned today...?

Not so fast. It is said the best lies are the ones that include a little truth and that's what Ralph is telling us here. A little truth mixed in with a little fiction. We call a meeting with the detectives and district attorney and set about updating everyone involved with all that we've found out so far.

First, there is the matter of the bedroom window. The evidence indicates that it was probably broken from the inside, not from the outside as was first claimed, casting doubt on Lisa's credibility. Glass particles were found on Lisa's bathrobe but not on Ralph's shoes. What the investigators want to know is how common are glass particles like these and how likely is it that Ralph's shoes *ought* to have glass on them if he broke the window? That's difficult to say. Some types of glass are quite common, especially the type that windows are made from. The blood on the shoes proves that Ralph was wearing these shoes at the scene, but we probably didn't recover the clothes he was wearing at the time. We would like to have looked for glass on those items. Lisa's bathrobe was recovered from a crime scene where glass was broken. The bathrobe may even have been on the floor under the window when it was broken.

Next there is the weak reaction of the seminal enzyme test. The bedding, both suspect and victim rape kits, Lisa's clothes and mattress all show no evidence of recent sexual activity. Lisa's rape kit shows enzyme levels more consistent with intercourse several days ago. As unlikely as it seems that Ralph left no hairs or semen on Lisa's clothes or bedding after such a violent rape, we can't prove there was no rape, since someone could use a condom and be able to get away clean.

Richard's blood is on the crowbar, the crowbar's paint on Richard's skull. The paint can't be matched like blood but it is similar in color and chemical properties. Again, how common is this kind of paint? We have also established that either the fire extinguisher found in the house or one chemically similar to it was used to fight the fire. The fingerprints show both Lisa and Ralph touched it. We can't tell how old fingerprints are and it's anyone's guess when they were deposited. The evidence supports a theory that Ralph did the actual killing and that Lisa was probably not even in the same room when it happened. The bloodstain patterns reveal this.

Comparing the scientific facts against theories advanced by both the defense and prosecution is difficult and each of our findings, taken out of context, proves very little. It's when they are taken together that they add up to a story. When testifying, we will be asked if a person could be reasonably expected to smash a window and climb through the broken glass without picking up microscopic glass chips on his shoes. In forming our opinion, we rely on experiments we have performed or professional articles we have read that relate to this type of situation. The jury must ultimately decide the reasonableness of the idea that it was Lisa or someone else who broke the window, not Ralph. Also, if we show a two-way transfer of evidence between the crowbar and the window frame, then how reasonable is it that some other object else did the damage? What is reasonable, not what is possible, is the standard.

Expert witness

Our role as expert witness separate us from other laboratory careers. Many technically challenging jobs involve procedures equally complex, but none offers the distinct challenge of defending the results in courts of law. It can be among the most stressful parts of our duties and at the same time the most rewarding. Here is where we reveal to the world what we've been doing quite literally in secret for weeks and months. Here's where our conclusions are challenged by other experts, our opinions dismissed by doubtful attorneys and, hopefully, we help the judge and jury find the truth.

When people hear the word expert they often think of a college professor with advanced degrees or maybe an author who gives well-attended lectures across the nation in his or her field of study. To most people, experts are people who surpasses all others in knowledge about a particular topic. In matters of law the term "expert" has a slightly different meaning.

Court trials are places where disputes are settled. There are at least three parties present, a plaintiff, defendant and trier of fact. In a criminal trial the plaintiff is the state, the defendant the one charged with a crime and the trier of fact could be a judge or jury, depending upon the wishes of the parties. The trier of fact decides which side should prevail depending upon the evidence presented. Witnesses are called to testify, sworn to tell the truth and asked questions about what they know. Witnesses must stick to what they know and not offer their opinions, with the singular exception of expert witnesses. The legal definition of who qualifies as an expert is much less rigid than the commonly held idea of an expert being the best in a given field. For court purposes, an expert is one who has knowledge not acquired by ordinary persons. A more specific definition might be:

> *...one who possess special skill or knowledge in some science, profession or business that is not common to the average man and is possessed by the expert by reason of his special study or experience.*

Whether a person possesses sufficient qualifications to be allowed to offer opinion testimony is up to the judge. The jury, however, is allowed to give appropriate weight to the testimony of each expert it hears. If a particular expert isn't very believable or has skimpy credentials, the jury may simply disregard his testimony even though the judge deemed him qualified to offer his opinion. Before the judge allows the expert to testify, each side has the right to quiz him or her about details regarding background, training, published papers, experience and education. After a witness has testified as an expert several times, the attorneys generally don't go through this much trouble; it's in the transcript of the previous trials and should not have changed much. The permanent record of a trial is a compelling reason for experts to give consistent opinions from one trial to the next. Opposing attorneys can and do request transcripts from previous trials to confront the witness with contradictory statements.

In cases involving the use of some new scientific procedure, criminalists can expect a real fight before being allowed to testify. In at least one case we know, a criminalist was not allowed to testify about a new procedure in advanced blood typing. Her testimony was abruptly restricted to what she actually did, her opinions not admitted into evidence. By ruling this way the judge forced the prosecutor to frantically seek another expert with a doctorate to come in and interpret the first criminalist's work. Could the first one have correctly interpreted it? Probably. Was the jury able to follow the Ph.D.'s testimony better than the first criminalist (who had a bachelor's degree)? We doubt it, but the judge felt he needed more "credibility" on the witness stand. In situations where research oriented hypothetical questions are posed to an expert witness, there's no doubt that more is better regarding the possession of advanced degrees.

The whole point of us testifying is to assist the jury in understanding the results of the tests we performed. If we as criminalists simply sat in the witness chair and told the jury exactly which tests we performed without offering our interpretation of what the results mean, they would have a difficult time making sense of it. We could be the greatest detective since Sherlock Holmes, the most thorough and dedicated since Edmond Locard, but if we have trouble communicating our findings to a jury, we're wasting a lot of effort. A much overlooked part of many criminalist's training is the ability to effectively present laboratory findings both orally and on paper.

The trial of the century

No book about forensic science would be complete without including the most famous forensic science case of our time, the O.J. Simpson criminal trial. O.J. Simpson, a famous football player, had been accused of slashing his ex-wife and a man to death in 1994. After a lengthy, much publicized trial, including a considerable amount of crime lab testimony, a jury acquitted him. In a later civil trial, another jury found him liable for the two deaths. Nearly a hundred books have been written about the various aspects of the trial and the lawyers involved that it almost seems pointless to add any more comments here. Almost. Only a few of the hundreds of authors and journalists writing about this sensational case have written from the unique point of being a forensic scientist.

The reverberations of this sensational case are only beginning to be felt in forensic science circles. Every aspect of evidence collection, storage and examination is now being scrutinized. We think that's great, as long as we remember one thing: The Simpson case was not like any case before or since. No matter how the evidence was handled, it probably wouldn't have affected the outcome. It would be a mistake to trade sound methods for untried methods out of the fear that another Simpson case might come along. Let's have change for improving methods and because it makes sense. If a method of blood collection, for example, is prone to contamination, we'll look for something better. But if a procedure is scientifically proven, should we abandon it out of fear of stiff cross examination?

Negative spin on criminalistics

It is perhaps unfortunate that most of the public's awareness of criminalistics as a profession was the result of the Simpson trial. Prior to that, when asked what it was that we did for our daily bread, our answers were met with puzzled glances, then an understanding look. "Oh, you mean like Quincy," the people would say. This is in reference to a TV show about a rogue medical examiner. "Oooh, that must be very interesting." We kind of enjoyed that obscurity, not realizing that we'd live to regret it. If juries have never heard of criminalistics, they are hard pressed to know how much weight to give the testimony of criminalists.

Well, they've heard of us now. Jurors in the Simpson case as well as millions of potential jurors across the country heard about sloppy collection practices, contamination, poor documentation and wrong conclusions. In what should have been our finest hour, we failed. There we were on T.V. broadcast worldwide with a golden opportunity to educate the public about criminalistics, and the public was eager to learn. We had a clean slate, now gone forever. Criminalists are not ones to toot their own horns, and the very personality traits that make them good criminalists, low key, calm and methodical, make them poor subjects for the drama-obsessed media. Our professionals came off looking substandard and ragged, littered with conflicting opinions. Honest scientific debate is a healthy thing, but when a few renegade members of the scientific community were given equal media exposure with views held by the vast majority, it was unfortunate no one was there to point out the imbalance. The public was left with a very clouded picture of criminalistics.

The good news is that when people have the opportunity to participate on a jury, they will have heard about complex tests like DNA and maybe these topics will be a little more familiar.

Today, the emotions about this case have cooled, and many people have become interested in criminalistics. In the end, maybe the trial will have served to inject new enthusiasm into the world of forensic science. Perhaps an influx of smart, young people who realize the importance of doing their jobs well, will join our ranks.

Unbiased witness

If the law has made you a witness,
remain a man of science.

You have no victim to avenge,
no guilty or innocent person to convict or save—
you must bear testimony within the limits of science.
—Dr. P. C. Brouardel
(A French forensic scientist, writing over a hundred years ago.)

It's particularly galling in court someone's remark implies that because we work for the police or the prosecution, we are biased and going to tip our interpretation to favor one side. True criminalists are only interested in what the evidence reveals, and become quite indignant when pressured, even slightly, to rush a report or skew results. Many of us view attorneys on both sides with some suspicion, and rather like it when the evidence comes out against someone's pet theory. The state has the prosecutor to look after the people's rights and the defendant has his team to make sure his rights are protected; we are the *only* advocates for the evidence. Future crime labs may be established under the purview of the court, not the prosecution or defense. This is how it works in certain European countries and it seems to avoid the parade of "experts," junk scientists and hired guns that have become so commonplace now.

An expert could be certified by the court, much like a foreign language translator is now, proving to the court's satisfaction that he or she is professionally qualified to offer opinions in addition to facts. Then, the evidence gathered at a crime scene would be examined by the court's expert and the findings presented. The fee the expert earned would be determined by the court as reasonable and customary. No one would, as happened in the Simpson trial, make $30,000 for watching the trial on television and testifying about crime lab procedures he'd never seen and only heard mentioned.

Valid opposition to this idea holds that the only way to keep the scientists honest, and therefore keep their findings correct is to allow referee analysis. This is where the same evidence is examined by an independent expert. Perhaps the court could have a list of approved referee scientists to render a second opinion. Whatever approach is taken, there needs to be less motivation for experts to disagree solely to generate a controversy resulting in increased fees. Juries have the impossible task of evaluating a witness' credibility based upon his or her testimony about subjects often beyond their experience. What else can they do but look at how the witnesses speak, see how they are dressed, listen to how they answer questions. A jury simply cannot evaluate the validity of the science, they must trust the court to exclude junk science (nonsense methods and conclusions disguised as legitimate research) and methods not accepted by the scientific community.

A smooth, well dressed, well spoken scientist can sell his point of view much more effectively than the stereotypical mousy, bespectacled lab researcher. The salesman's science may be shaky and his methods unsound, but he is given equal time to refute the opposing expert. The dedicated researcher, spurning the thousand-dollar suit, may have carefully reached a brilliant conclusion but if he can't sell it to the jury, he might as well have stayed home.

School's out

Teaching the jury can be at once frustrating and rewarding. The courtroom is a most artificial environment in that all of the information is presented in an awkward style with constant interruption. We are not allowed to ask the jury questions as we could in a classroom. A teacher asks questions and gets answers to establish the students' understanding. Questions and answers, back and forth, if a student is not clear, a teacher can explain the concept in a different way. People on a jury are expected to get it the first time they hear it. At least that's the way it seems. Occasionally a juror realizes how important a point might be and writes a question for the criminalist on a piece of paper and hands it to the bailiff, who hands it to the judge. If the judge approves, he will ask the witness. We have to rely on subtle clues from the jury to evaluate how well we are connecting with them. Bored looks, snickers and fidgeting can all signal that the testimony is getting too technical, or that it's been too long since the last break.

Pushing the limits

We have described several different methods of analysis, some of them incredibly sensitive. DNA tests are being developed that can amplify the DNA from just a single cell. Drug detection methods have been refined to the point of being able to detect invisible traces of cocaine on paper money or find morphine in the urine of a person whose only crime was to eat a poppy-seed muffin or two. As our ability to detect traces of chemicals improves, a new question is beginning to form. Are we sure we ought to be reporting such small quantities? Let's first think about what the result means before we think we've made a criminal association. In a case of arson, if we detect traces of gasoline on a suspect's shoes, could he have recently filled his car with gas and dropped a single drop of gasoline on his shoes from replacing the pump? We have methods that can detect very small amounts of gasoline quite easily. If we find cocaine on a wad of money, could it be traces rubbed off from some money that got contaminated from still other money? We have methods which can detect that, too. When applied to an ordinary shirt front, the saliva mapping described in the first chapter identifies lots of spatter from simply talking and eating normally. Might some of that flying spit contain epithelial cells, each containing DNA? It does. Could someone working at the crime scene have forgotten to wear gloves when handling the evidence? In the crime lab we may even need to wear a face mask when working around evidence. It would be useful to know the DNA types of every person who handled the evidence to be able to eliminate them when the DNA test results of a piece of evidence are reported, similar to the way it is done with fingerprints.

In testing body fluids for drugs, there's a concept known as cutoff limit. We know that we can detect tiny amounts of drugs in urine and blood, but we arbitrarily set a limit low enough to render meaningful results, but high enough to avoid picking up innocent background. This means that we could go lower and maybe find drugs, but there would be some uncertainty in the meaning of the result. At such low levels, we might have reached the limits of detection for one test but be well within the limits of another, not unlike the conflict we mentioned between the differing levels of sensitivity of the arson dog and the crime lab.

Errors and omissions

Mistakes happen all the time, little errors such as not using fresh test solutions, or not cleaning up a sample before running it on the IR. Because more things don't match than do, these little mistakes usually lead to what is termed a false exclusion. This means that the unknown evidence sample is incorrectly concluded as having no connection to a crime scene. Another example occurs when old, outdated test solutions are used. Take the example of mapping Lisa's bed sheet for semen stains.

The test solution, MUP, ages quickly and is no longer effective when it gets old. To avoid this problem we run a tiny patch of known semen on a piece of absorbent paper with the test solution first. If that comes out OK, then we are confident the solution is still good.

If only it were a perfect world. All of our tests would be specific, all criminalists would be well trained, well spoken and proceed with all due caution before announcing test results. Of course we are human and make mistakes, but knowing this we design our procedures to catch mistakes before they escape from the lab resulting in an erroneous report. Some mistakes are harmless like forgetting to put paper in the GC's printer. Other mistakes are more serious like forgetting to run controls. It's how a person handles a mistake that really counts. Do they hide it, fabricating a lab report? Or do they "come clean," and issue an amended lab report acknowledging the error and correcting it.

Of the thousands of dedicated professionals working in the forensic sciences a few bad apples have been discovered. A few have been caught "dry labbing," where evidence isn't really examined but results are written anyway. A few others have been found to have been incompetent, incorrectly performing tests that they don't understand, even after having received training. One or two have been exposed as outright frauds, testifying to practically anything the prosecutor or detectives wanted to hear. When they are caught, they are marked forever. Their testimony and reports are matters of record and often shared among other prosecutors. If they used to work for us and turn up in another jurisdiction, we might get a panicked phone call from some district attorney wanting everything we know about the "expert." Credibility is the only thing a criminalist really has and once lost, it cannot be easily recovered.

Quality assured

The problem of assuring a high-quality product is tough. We're sure that if we as criminalists don't address it ourselves the government is sure to do it for us—with regulation. Hospital labs have already had to cope with governmental guidelines and inspections aimed at reducing error rates and improving accuracy. Crime labs are in a unique situation in that they have no control over the history of the samples they accept. Hospital laboratories know exactly where their samples came from and where to get more if they need it. Crime labs practically never know

where their samples came from or how old they are. We're the ones who are supposed to figure that out.

We subscribe to a program of proficiency testing for the laboratory. A commercial testing company prepares a hypothetical case and evidence which might have been recovered such as paint or fire debris. The evidence is sealed up and sent to participating labs. The "case" is assigned to a criminalist who works on it, prepares and sends a report back to the company. The findings of all of the participating labs are published anonymously so that we all can see how other labs operate.

In addition to laboratory-wide proficiency testing, there is personal testing. Individual criminalists may decide to become board-certified by a group offering a test in their subject area. Our favorite is the American Board of Criminalists, the ABC. This group has devoted much time, money and effort into developing a well designed, fair certification exam that tests the applicant's knowledge, skills and abilities in general criminalistics. The successful applicant is termed a Diplomate. For those

Richard T. Nowitz/Corbis

Fifth graders discover the world of the microscope. A strong program of early science education is the best investment we can make in the future of forensic science.

wishing to go further, a Fellow's exam is available in specialty areas such as fire debris analysis or DNA testing. In addition to taking a more difficult exam, Fellows must participate in personal proficiency testing every year. They are sent evidence just like the lab-wide proficiency testing only it is they alone who must perform the analysis. Both Diplomates and Fellows must renew their certification every five years by accumulating a number of professional development and participation credits. These are earned by publishing papers, giving lectures and attending classes in forensic science.

Accreditation

Beyond the personal certification of individual criminalists, there is a group that inspects entire laboratories, reviewing procedures, policies and the laboratory setup and building itself. The American Society of Crime Laboratory Directors Laboratory Accreditation Board (ASCLD-LAB) has taken on this enormous task in an effort to provide a means of assuring a credible, quality product emerging from the crime labs in this country. Before being inspected, a lab gets ready for the big day by overhauling and revising analytical methods and safety procedures. Manuals outlining every aspect of running a crime lab are written and edited. Case notes are checked for completeness and evidence handling methods are carefully reviewed. The lab is spit-polished and presented for the most rigorous inspection in its history. During the actual inspection, case notes and procedure manuals may be demanded and given close scrutiny. The rewards of passing this white-glove test are many. People want assurances that the food they eat, the medicines they take, indeed every item they consume are clean and free from defects. Until recently, crime labs were islands in a sea of quality assurance regulation. No longer can we avoid the inevitable trend toward verifiable accountability. If, during inspection, we notice equipment that needs upgrading, a section which needs better trained personnel, we need to allocate enough money and effort to correct the problem before wrong conclusions are reached or actual casework is adversely affected.

What does it take to be a criminalist?

A criminalist is a person who is an independent thinker, with a curious mind and vigorous in his or her search for truth. These are the qualities we hope every criminalist will bring to the profession. The lazy

need not apply. A four-year degree in one of the natural sciences, chemistry, physics, biology, is a great starting point. Specializing too early in forensic sciences courses may diminish a student's employment opportunities if few crime lab jobs are available at graduation. Volunteering or working in a crime lab as a lab technician or intern will give the prospective criminalist a foot in the door when a position becomes available. Science fair participation at the junior high and high school level are excellent training opportunities for the would-be scientist. Exposing elementary school students to science is essential in preparing an inquiring mind, one in which science is seen not as wizardry, but as a way of understanding the world around us.

Several groups of professional criminalists around the world have formed to promote the sharing of information, techniques and methods with their peers. Among these, the California Association of Criminalists (CAC) has often taken the lead in providing training, education and information about job opportunities to scores of would-be criminalists. In addition, there is the American Academy of Forensic Sciences (AAFS), and numerous regional associations including the Northwest Association of Forensic Scientists (NWAFS), the Southern Assoc. of Forensic Scientists (SAFS), Mid-Atlantic Assoc. of Forensic Scientists (MAAFS), Northeast Assoc. of Forensic Scientists (NEAFS), Southwest Association of Forensic Scientists (SWAFS), Midwestern Assoc. of Forensic Scientists, Inc. (MAFS) and the International Assoc. of Forensic Sciences (IAFS).

What remains

There are many topics left to explore in the field of criminalistics that we didn't cover. There are scientists specializing in the areas of soil comparison, hair examination, bullet trajectory analysis, accident scene reconstruction, questioned document examination, and mitochondrial DNA testing to name only a few. The field is alive and expanding into new areas every day, limited only by the imagination of the scientist and the needs of the case.

FOR FURTHER STUDY

Criminalistics : An Introduction to Forensic Science

by Richard Saferstein

6th Edition

Prentice Hall, 1997

ISBN: 0135929407

Forensic Science : An Introduction to Criminalistics

by Peter DeForest

McGraw Hill Text, 1983

ISBN: 0070162670

An Introduction to Forensic DNA Analysis

by Keith Inman and Norah Rudin

CRC Press, 1997

ISBN: 0849381177

The Century of the Detective

by Jurgen Thorwald

Hartcourt, Brace and World, Inc., New York, 1965

Crime and Science

by Jurgen Thorwald

Hartcourt, Brace and World, Inc., New York, 1967

The Encyclopedia of Forensic Science

by Brian Lane

Headline Book Publishing, PLC, London, 1992

Hard Evidence

by David Fisher

Simon and Schuster, New York, 1995

CLUES! A History of Forensic Detection

by Colin Wilson

Warner Books, Inc., USA 1991

American Academy of Forensic Sciences

410 N. 21st Street, Ste. 203

P.O. Box 669

Colorado Springs, CO 80901-0669

http://www.criminalistics.com

ACKNOWLEDGMENTS

The author is indebted to the following persons and institutions:

Edwin L. Jones, Jr. and James Roberts, Margaret Schaeffer and Michael Parigian; Raymond J. Davis; Dom Denio, Federal Bureau of Investigation, Washington, D.C.; Wayne Moorehead; Vince Vitale; Loye Barton; Judith Cox; Joe Hourigan; Raymond Davis, California Association of Criminalists; Terry Spear and John DeHaan, California Criminalistics Institute, Sacramento; Walter C. McCrone, McCrone Research Institute; Keith Mashburn, Ventura County Fire Department; Al Milner, Ojai Printing and Publishing; Karen Stedman, One-On-One Book Productions; E. J. Wagner; Richard Saferstein; American Academy of Forensic Sciences; The American Board of Criminalistics.

Index

PICTURE CREDITS

ABOUT THE AUTHOR

JOHN HOUDE, B.S., D.A.B.C, is a board certified, twenty-year veteran criminalist and the author of over twenty articles on the subject of forensic science. His articles have appeared in such publications as *The California Narcotic Officer* and the *Journal of Forensic Sciences*. He is in his seventh year as publisher of the *CACNews*, the quarterly journal of the California Association of Criminalists, representing over 500 criminalists worldwide. John has spent much of his career educating juries, investigators and attorneys in various topics of forensic science. His specialty areas include the analysis of narcotics, trace and fire debris evidence. John lives in Southern California with his wife Donna.